COOKING

VEGETARIAN

VESANTO MELINA, R.D.

JOSEPH FOREST

MACMILLAN CANADA
TORONTO

Canadian Cataloguing in Publication Data

Melina, Vesanto, 1942–
  Cooking vegetarian : recipes inspired by the bestselling Becoming vegetarian

Includes index.
ISBN 0-7715-7391-X

 1. Vegetarian cookery.   I. Forest, Joseph.   II. Title.
TX837.M45   1996   641.5'636   C96-931064-1

3 4 5 — 00 99 98

Cover and text design by Counterpunch

Cover illustration by Helen D'Souza

Type Composition by IBEX Graphic Communications Inc.

Macmillan Canada wishes to thank the Canada Council and the Ontario Ministry of Culture and Communications for supporting its publishing program.

Macmillan Canada
A Division of Canada Publishing Corporation
Toronto, Ontario, Canada

Printed in Canada

Contents

Vesanto's dedication
To David, who touches, inspires and makes me laugh every day.
Thank you for sharing my life journey.

Joseph's dedication
To the Spirit of Guidance

and

To the loving memory of my father and brother,
Jean-Paul and Philippe Forest.

ACKNOWLEDGMENTS

Our deepest thanks to: David Melina for patient and enduring assistance with the nutritional analysis and for clarity in giving feedback, Debrah Rafel for her editing, evaluation of recipes and their development and her precious love, wisdom and support throughout this project.

Much love to our dear friends who supported the vision in a myriad of ways: Michael Fisher, chef and dear colleague, for his ideas, suggestions and recipe contributions, Jean Golden for thoughtful assistance with text, Lance Shaler for his valuable insight and Jean-Pierre and Kate Ross LeBlanc for their ideas.

We would like to extend our appreciation to our skillful editors, Kirsten Hanson, Susan Lawrence, Shannon Potts and the great staff at Macmillan Canada including Ann Nelles, Sheron Metcalfe, Susan Girvan, Karen O'Reilly and Mike Richardson.

We are grateful to the registered dietitians who unfailingly offered us their expertise and provided invaluable assistance when asked: Carollyne Conlinn, Brenda Davis, Victoria Harrison and Jean Fremont.

Many thanks to those who assisted in recipe testing and development: Carol Sue Hunting, Francis Janes, Bianca Molinari, Nancy and Paul Travis and Georgina Seifert, Delta Nutrition Systems, Junko Valle, Sheila Hoffman, Debrah Gallie and Elysa Markowitz.

Thanks to the following authors and friends who allowed us to use recipes from their books: Rynn Berry, author of *Famous*

Vegetarians and Their Favorite Recipes, Pythagorean Publishers, New York; Ron Pickarski, author of *Friendly Foods* and *Eco-Cuisine*, Ten Speed Press, Berkeley; Joanne Stepaniak, author of *The Uncheese Book* and *Table for Two*, The Book Publishing Company, Summertown, and Mollie Katzen, author of *The Moosewood Cookbook*, Ten Speed Press, Berkeley.

We are grateful to those that generously provided outstanding products for recipe testing: Dwayne and Doreen Smith of Grain-Works Inc.; Martha Johnson, Lynette Renner, Cyndi Eicholz and Mary Scott of Eden Foods; Kelly Smith of Frontier Herbs; Tom McReynolds of Morinauga Foods; Aaran Stevens and John Anthony of Nature's Path Foods; Omega Nutrition Canada; Sunrise Soya Foods; Yves Potvin of Yves Veggie Cuisine; Red Star Nutritional Yeast/Universal Foods and Asian Family Foods and Artesian Acres.

We appreciate the fine technical support provided by: Scott Huiskens and Chris Gramlich of ESHA Research in connection with The Food Processor nutritional analysis program and Elisabeth Hands for introducing us to this excellent program.

Sincere thanks to everyone who made the photography for the book possible: Larry Nowakowski, Amy Huebner and R. Steve Martin of Universal Foods; Diane Jang, Marcia Pong and Peter Joe of Sunrise Soya Foods; Sally Gralla of Eden Foods; Robert Gaffney and Amber Hall of Omega Nutrition Canada; Adonis Photography; Antique and Old Lace; Belinda Wheatley, food stylist; Ross Durant Photography; the B.C Blueberry Council; Home Economist Linda Braun and the Saskatchewan Pulse Crop Development Board, Laurie Jones of Whalebone Production and Al Reid.

Special thanks to: Michael Theodore and Gail Mountain for their assistance with the appendix, and Jean-Marc · Fulsack for his inspiration and to Jae Choi.

We also offer our heartfelt appreciation and thanks to: Dr. E.S. Goranson, Vesanto's father, an outstanding teacher and scientist; Aldona Goranson, Vesanto's stepmother, a wonderful cook and deeply inspiring woman; Louise Forest, Joseph's mother, for her unconditional love and guidance.

FOREWORD

Nothing will benefit human health and increase the chances for survival on earth as much as the evolution to a vegetarian diet.

Albert Einstein

An emerging force is gaining momentum within our culture, a force both powerful and healing. It is the shift towards a plant-based diet.

The advantages to be gained by this shift are so multidimensional that they are being recognized by groups throughout our culture. Agricultural economists, environmentalists and school children are aware that we maximize our limited land and water resources when we center our diets lower on the food chain. Dietitians, physicians, scientific experts and the general public are acknowledging that the diet centered on animal products that has been ours in this century has proven to be a choice linked with chronic disease.

Looking after one's personal health has become a driving force for baby boomers and for a significant proportion of adults in all age groups. Vegetarian eating is not a passing fad but a preference that's here to stay. As you walk along supermarket aisles, you see people studying food labels, considering the fat content, sodium levels, presence or absence of animal products and other ingredients. Items most of us had never heard of 15 years ago, such as tofu, veggie burgers and organic produce, are the thriving businesses of the '90s and are showing up on supermarket shelves as well as on the menus of mainstream restaurants. A plant-based diet is gaining the respect of international health organizations, national governments and the medical establishment.

My own journey with vegetarianism began as a teenager and has continued to this day. I have personally experienced the shift from being on the fringe with dietary choices in my own profession, to becoming one of a growing number with the same preference.

On a day-to-day basis, what inspires some people, and not others, to change? Some change motivators are: concern about health or fear of disease; awareness of the billions of animals being processed in the factory farming system; and a sense of responsibility towards the earth's resources. At the same time, people prefer foods that are familiar, and feel nurtured by dishes that have been lifelong favorites. Through the book *Healthy Pleasures: Great Tastes from Canadian Dietitians and Chefs*, I am a strong supporter of the work of dietitians and chefs across Canada who have been trend setters in the new way of eating. However good the nutritional analysis looks on paper, people are drawn to the meal that is bursting with good flavor. Whether conscious choice or familiar habit, the food we eat must taste good.

For nutritionists and culinary experts, the taste transition is clear . . . and here are two professionals who have risen to the challenge. Vesanto and Joseph have taken the steps many others will follow – using their professional knowledge and communications skills to create a blueprint for culinary change.

Whether you are parents struggling to counteract the impact of some advertising on the diets of your growing children, teenagers trying to convince Mom that a plant-based diet will not result in permanent health damage, or professionals faced with clients who want change but don't know quite where to start – this book is for you. A perfect companion to Melina and co-authors' handbook to a plant-based diet, *Becoming Vegetarian*, this volume brings the science of nutrition alive in the kitchen.

I am pleased and honored to recommend *Cooking Vegetarian* to change-makers with exceptionally good taste, in all walks of life.

Carollyne Conlinn, RDN, FCDA
Past President (1995), Canadian Dietetic Association
Vice President, Health Care, Versa Services

Two Words from the Authors

A word from Vesanto

I was fascinated by the field of dietetics due to a delight in working with food and a pleasure in scientific exploration. Both of my parents were outstanding teachers at the University of British Columbia and I followed their examples by teaching nutrition to students in dietetics and home economics on the UBC faculty for six years. My early training, teaching and personal eating patterns were based on the traditional four food groups, with meals centered around animal products.

The non-academic sides of life offered me different perspectives. After the birth of my son, Chris, and daughter, Kavyo, I had the opportunity to live on an immense cattle ranch, travel around the world several times and live in India and Nepal for four years. During these years I learned a great deal about the production and preparation of food in many cultures, and the seeds were planted for the vegetarian ways of eating that I have followed since 1978.

My initial attraction to a vegetarian diet was enjoyment of the food itself, shared with friends in Canada and many parts of the globe. My daughter has been a lifelong vegetarian and my son began cooking early and developed a fine sense of the use of spices and seasonings. Food preparation has long been a comforting, creative activity to do alone, as well as a pleasurable way to spend time in the kitchen with family and friends.

Over time, the profound significance of our food choices on the environment and health, and the ethical issues involved, have led me to make vegetarian nutrition and foods central to my professional career. In doing the extensive research for *Becoming Vegetarian* I came to see that not only could we get all the nutrients we need in a plant-based diet but that such a diet makes a great deal of sense from the same perspectives (health, environment and ethics). My own way of eating has become totally plant-based (vegan). Because the process has been a gradual dietary evolution over the years, it has afforded me an understanding of challenges and solutions for those anywhere on the continuum between near-vegetarian through to vegan.

I have seen a shift in attitude among those at the forefront of the dietetics profession, from an earlier attitude that vegetarian diets are nutritionally risky, to an awareness that greater risks of chronic disease are associated with the heavily meat- and dairy-centered diet of most North Americans. Following the publication of *Becoming Vegetarian* I have had the honor in my profession of receiving the prestigious Clintec award for leadership in dietetics.

Once I teamed up with Joseph Forest, the sensory appeal of food in my nutrition presentations took a quantum leap, and delicious took on new meaning. Joseph has been a wonderful teacher for me, sharing the unique perspectives of a chef as well as being a truly inspirational human being.

A word from Joseph

From an early age I have been mysteriously drawn to food. My first formal experience with it began at 13 while working as a baker's assistant for three years. Although, at 16, the thought of a career in the arena of food was not a consideration, it seemed this destiny would continue to draw me forward.

When I was 17, my father died of a massive heart attack. For years I had watched him ignore his doctor's advice regarding the risks of certain foods. When reminded of this at home, he would act as though he knew better and shrug off any sense of danger. His untimely death at 51 had a very significant impact on me. So having witnessed the correlation between diet and disease, I began to investigate the other side of the coin – the healing power of foods.

My inquiry eventually led to formal chef training. I enrolled initially to deepen my understanding of food and to improve my cooking skills. However, by graduation I had acknowledged my strong, intuitive gift with food and only then did I decide to embark upon a career as a professional chef in fine dining restaurants and hotels.

During the course of my career, I often contemplated my father's death. At work my duties involved preparing and serving many of the rich and fatty foods that my father had been advised to reduce or eliminate. I knew in my heart that I was contributing to the health problems of the nation. This created a discrepancy in my life until I eventually left the restaurant and hotel industry to work with the foods I now believe have a more beneficial impact on our bodies and our planet.

Over the many years that I have worked with natural whole foods, three personal perspectives have emerged.

1. Transition from one dietary lifestyle to another can take years. For lasting results, this important process requires time.

2. Since each person is constitutionally different, no one diet is good for everyone. Although we all need carbohydrates, protein, vitamins and minerals, the combinations of foods we choose in the process of meeting those needs are as varied as the people of earth, and will change from one stage of life to another.

3. We are all brilliantly tailored individuals, guided by a deep source of inner intelligence. If we pay attention to the wisdom of our bodies we will be led into the dietary pattern that best serves who we are as individuals.

The recipes in this book were developed according to the tastes and preferences of the authors. It is our sincere wish that you will derive joy from them in good health. As you work with and adapt this book to suit your lifestyle, be prepared to learn, eat, enjoy and laugh.

CHAPTER ONE

HEALTHY, DELICIOUS AND EASY

The scrumptious aroma of baking potatoes when you return home.

Sensuous scents wafting through the kitchen, as onions and garlic roast in the oven.

The glorious green of lightly steamed broccoli, the glistening ruby red of sweet peppers.

The juicy crunch of your first mouthful of a toasted sandwich, heaped with fresh tomato slices.

The explosion of flavor, the sweet tartness when you bite into a warm cranberry muffin.

Oh, the pleasures of savory food. When it comes to nutrition, are you accustomed to thinking that if it's healthy, it probably doesn't taste good? Let go of that idea right now! The dishes that tempt us with their sensuous appeal can be the same nutritious vegetarian dishes that promote our well-being. As our health consciousness increases, we don't want fat- and cholesterol-laden foods that can be described as "a heart attack on a plate". We're looking for a marriage of flavor *along with* good-quality ingredients. That's exactly what the following recipes provide.

In the creative collaboration of the two authors of this book, the words *healthy, delicious and easy* have been central themes for the foods we prepare. These three words have been both challenge and inspiration. Recipes have had to qualify on all three counts. Our vision has been to create appetizing and nourishing dishes that can be assembled by people with full and busy lives.

In this chapter, we introduce the nutritional guidelines that serve as foundation for the menus and recipes that follow. The Vegetarian Food Guide on page 3 was modeled after national food guides developed by dietitians and other nutritional experts in Canada, the United States, Great Britain, Australia and New Zealand. It retains the strengths of these national food guides and provides a solid basis for planning your diet, menus and shopping lists. For more detailed nutrition information about vegetarian eating, see *Becoming Vegetarian* by dietitians Vesanto Melina, Brenda Davis and Victoria Harrison, published by Macmillan Canada.

The Vegetarian Food Guide is a user-friendly way of ensuring that you get all the nutrients you need for great health. Nutrients are food components that help nourish the body, that is provide energy, serve as building materials, help maintain or repair the body or support growth. Nutrients include protein (with nine essential amino acids), carbohydrate, essential fatty acids, 13 vitamins, more than 16 minerals and water. In this guide, foods that are similar nutritionally, and that provide many of the same vitamins and minerals, are grouped together. Foods are divided into the following four categories:

> *grain products*
> *vegetables & fruits*
> *milk & alternatives*
> *beans & alternatives*

An additional category, not included in the guide, is *extras*, the foods that are high in fat or sugar or have little nutritional merit.

Vegetarian diets range from lacto-ovo-vegetarian (including dairy products and eggs) to vegan (no foods of animal origin), with many variations. Our emphasis here is to provide a sound nutritional framework that can be adapted for many vegetarian ways of eating. Whatever pattern you have chosen, it is important to make choices regularly from all of the food groups, because each group contributes individual components to help you maintain top physical condition.

In practice, the system becomes elegantly simple. Just select a few foods from each group to meet the recommended number of servings. An easy way to remember the minimum number of servings of food groups named from left to right across the bottom of

Vegetarian Food Guide

Also include sources of:
- **vitamin B12 (food or supplement)**
- **vitamin D (sunlight, fortified food or supplement)**

and

- **omega-3 fatty acids (such as flaxseed oil, canola oil, walnuts, tofu)**

BREADS
Bread, 1 slice
Roll, bagel, pita, tortilla, chapati, roti, bannock, scone, hamburger bun or hot dog bun, 1

HOT / COLD CEREALS
Cooked cereal, 3/4 cup
Dry cereal, 1 oz.

VEGETABLE / FRUIT
Such as potato, carrot, tomato, apple, banana, orange, peach, 1 medium

SMALL VEGETABLE / FRUIT
Such as apricots, plums, 2

GREENS
Broccoli, kale, Chinese cabbage, bok choy, okra, 1 cup cooked/ 2 cups raw
Dry hijiki seaweed, 1/4 cup

PASTA / GRAINS
Cooked, 1 cup

VEGETABLE / FRUIT
Fresh, frozen, cooked, 1/2 cup

LEGUMES / TOFU
White, navy, great northern, black turtle beans, 1 cup
Tofu with calcium, 1/4 cup

LEGUMES / TOFU
Cooked beans, peas, lentils, 1/2–1 cup
Tofu, 1/3 cup

NUTS
Almond butter, 3–4 tbsp

MEAT SUBSTITUTES / ANALOGUES / TEMPEH
1 serving / patty

OTHER
Muffin, pancake, waffle, 1 small / 1/2 large
Wheat germ, 2 tbsp
Crackers, 2–6

VEGETABLE / FRUIT JUICE
1/2 cup

DAIRY PRODUCTS
Milk, yogurt, 1/2 cup
Cheese, 1/2–1 oz.

NUTS / SEEDS, 3–4 tbsp

FIGS, 5

NUT / SEED BUTTER, 2–3 tbsp

SALAD
1 cup

BLACKSTRAP MOLASSES, 1 tbsp

EGG, 1–2

BEVERAGES FORTIFIED with 150 mg calcium / serving

SOY MILK, 1 cup

GRAIN PRODUCTS	**VEGETABLES & FRUITS**	**MILK & ALTERNATIVES**	**BEANS & ALTERNATIVES**
5 to 12 servings / day	5 to 10 servings / day	4 to 6 servings / day	2 to 4 servings / day

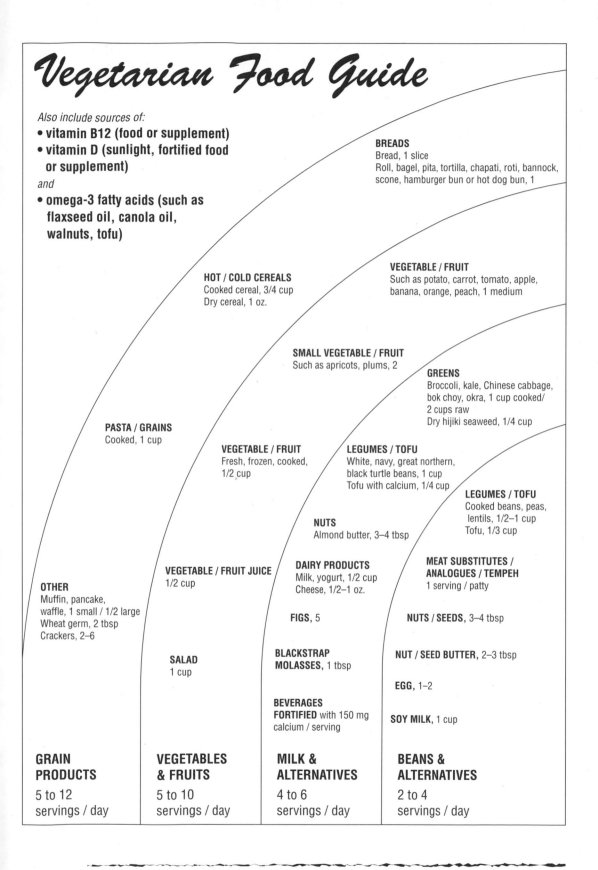

the guide is to think of the pattern 5, 5, 4, 2. The guide is for a typical day's intake; however, this can be averaged over a few days.

Similarities and differences within each food group

While foods in the same group have certain similarities in their concentrations of carbohydrate, protein, vitamins and minerals, the nutritional profile of each food is unique. To illustrate this, a common feature of foods in the Beans & Alternatives group is that they have significant amounts of protein, iron, zinc, magnesium and certain B vitamins. At the same time, the individual foods within each group offer distinct differences nutritionally.

For example, tofu and other soy products provide us with substantial quantities of omega-3 fatty acids. We require these essential fatty acids for building cell membranes and for certain beneficial hormone-like substances called prostaglandins. Soybeans and their products also contain the phytochemicals (plant chemicals) called isoflavones, which appear to have protective qualities against cancer.

Lentils, peas and a variety of beans are similar to soybeans in providing plenty of protein and trace minerals. But these other legumes differ from soybeans in that they are very low in fat – and in essential fatty acids.

In this same food group, nuts and seeds are extremely high in fat. In moderation, nut and seed butters can be valuable for growing children and for others with high energy needs. For additional benefit, if you choose almonds or sesame seeds, you'll be getting a calcium-rich food. If you munch on cashews, you'll obtain plenty of zinc, and walnuts are an excellent source of omega-3 fatty acids.

So, choose an average of two servings from the Beans & Alternatives group daily, and vary your choices. Variety will make your meals interesting and help you get all the nutrients you need.

Complementary protein: theme from a bygone era

In the early 1970s, protein complementation (combining plant foods such as grains and legumes to ensure intake of all essential amino acids) was considered a necessary part of vegetarian meal planning. This concept, now outdated, was based on animal research that underestimated the nutritional value of plant protein for humans. Subsequent research has clearly established that when we take in sufficient calories and consume an assortment of the foods shown in the Vegetarian Food Guide, we have little difficulty getting all the amino acids needed to build top-quality protein. You can continue to eat that savory pea soup *with* fresh bread, or sweet and sour tofu *with* steaming rice, but combine these foods because they're delightful together, not because you *need* to combine the proteins at the same meal!

When you make your selections within each food group, you'll find that there can be quite a range in quality. As much as possible, choose fresh foods that have been minimally processed, grown without harmful pesticides, and prepare them to preserve their nutrients.

Grain products: the energy foods

The breads, cereals, rice, pasta and other foods in this group are central to your energy supply. Grains are parcels of energy from the sun, stored in the form of complex carbohydrates (starch). Packaged along with carbohydrate are the B vitamins, which help release this energy. If you look at Table 1.3 on page 13, you will see that grains also provide protein, in amounts very close to those recommended for our overall dietary intake (Table 1.1). In fact, 47% of the world's human protein needs and 51% of our calories (energy) come from grains. As shown in the Vegetarian Food Guide, the minimum number of daily servings recommended for most adults is five. Keep in mind that in many meals, you are likely to eat several servings of grain products, for example, two slices of bread in a sandwich or several cups of steaming pasta.

Whole compared with refined grains

The outer layers (bran) and the inner core (germ) of whole grains are concentrated sources of trace minerals: iron, zinc, magnesium, chromium and many more. When grains are refined, the bran and germ are removed. In the process, most of the trace minerals, many vitamins such as folate and vitamin E, and the bulk of the fiber are lost. Thus, the recipes in this book focus on whole grains and use of refined products has been kept to a minimum.

In your shift toward a plant-based diet, one adjustment that may help you a great deal is to change your concept of what constitutes a meal. In the 20th century, much to the discomfort of their coronary arteries, people in North America and Europe became accustomed to meals centered around meat, fish and poultry. This way of dining has been a fairly recent development in the history of mankind's culinary adventures, and can be viewed as an experiment that is showing poor results. The eating patterns of most of our ancestors were based on plant foods, and this pattern is still found on the majority of dinner tables throughout the world. In the 1990s, leading health experts advocate a return to complex carbohydrates. Rice, pasta and other grains are reclaiming a central place in North American meals and menus.

While cereal foods have an important role to play as providers of energy, B vitamins and trace minerals, grains are deficient in vitamins A and C, and that leads us to the next important food group.

Vegetables and fruits: nature's healers, the protective foods

You probably learned in grade school that fruits and vegetables provide us with vitamin C. The yellow, orange, red and green foods in this group are also rich in beta-carotene, the brightly colored form of vitamin A in plant foods. Vitamins C and A are antioxidants. They protect us from the damaging effects of free radicals, which are destructive chemicals in our bodies that set up chain reactions, leading to disease. Currently there is an explosion of interest among scientists in common vegetables and fruits. This is due to the discovery and identification of a vast array of phytochemicals with protective value far beyond that of vitamins.

The foods in this group tend to be excellent sources of folate, a vitamin required to make new cells (of prime importance during pregnancy). Vegetables and fruits are noted for their absence of fat (avocados and olives are exceptions).

You'll get added health benefits when you eat a vitamin C-rich vegetable or fruit at the same meal with an item from the Beans & Alternatives group. That's because the vitamin C interacts with the iron in beans (or other foods in this group), making the iron two to three times as available for absorption. Vegetables that are particularly helpful, since they provide more than 30 mg of vitamin C in a 1/2-cup (125 mL) serving, are broccoli, brussels sprouts, cabbage, cauliflower, collards, kale, kohlrabi, peppers and snow peas. Fruits that are excellent sources of vitamin C are cantaloupe, citrus fruits and juices, guava, kiwifruit, papaya, strawberries and vitamin C-fortified juices. Combinations that help iron absorption are not unusual or difficult to assemble – in fact, they are present in many familiar recipes. You are helping your iron absorption by adding chopped onions to pea soup or tomatoes to baked beans. The combination of fruit with tofu in the Fruit Shake on page 36 has the same effect.

Milk & Alternatives

In North America, we tend to think of milk and milk products as *the* calcium foods. This is likely a consequence of TV advertising and plenty of educational materials provided by the dairy boards during our schooling. While milk is *one* of the sources of this mineral, many population groups have excellent lifelong bone health while relying on a variety of plant foods as their primary contributors of dietary calcium.

It is important to note that many dietary and lifestyle factors contribute to strong bones. Among these are regular weight-bearing exercise, a diet with many bone-building nutrients, adequate calcium intake, avoiding cigarette smoking and avoiding a diet that causes calcium loss (too much salt, alcohol and protein, especially animal protein).

The plant foods that supply dietary calcium are shown in the second arch from the right in the Vegetarian Food Guide. Although dairy products are included in this group, our emphasis is on plant sources of calcium, which tend to be less familiar to people. Many people would benefit by adding more of these foods to their diets. Some people drink milk on occasion, but much less than the quantities recommended in national food guides (2 cups/500 mL of milk or equivalent amounts of milk products daily). Other people skip dairy foods altogether, but do not include alternatives, often because they don't know which plant foods are calcium-rich.

In this book, menus and recipes emphasize using calcium-rich foods in a wide variety of tasty and easy ways originating from around the globe. The nutritional notes below many recipes show them to be a *source* of calcium. This means that one serving provides between 55 and 164 mg calcium. Where a food is listed as a *good source*, it means that a serving provides between 165 and 274 mg calcium; an *excellent source* contains more than 275 mg. (The recommended intake for women up to age 49 is 700 mg per day; for older women and for men the recommended intake is 800 mg.) Your absorption of calcium is relatively efficient when you take in moderate amounts over the course of a day.

Among the recipes you will find delicious and attractive ways to serve black turtle beans, and the white beans also known as navy or great northern. Tofu can be an excellent calcium source as calcium salts are often used in tofu production. To make sure the tofu you buy is made with calcium, check the ingredient list on the label for calcium. These and other Milk Alternatives in the Vegetarian Food Guide could become mighty contributors to your bone health.

Broccoli and kale (dark green members of the cabbage family) and the light green Chinese cabbage (also known as napa cabbage or *sui choy*) have shot to popularity in recent years. Once they were the butt of jokes, and were served as overcooked and unwelcome parts of dinner. Now photos of these deep or pale green vegetables grace the food sections of newspapers and magazines. One reason is research proving the exceptionally high availability to the body of the calcium present in these greens. Other valuable features are the presence of healthful antioxidants and of phytochemicals that can help block the development of cancers.

Some calcium-rich foods are very low in fat: figs, greens, hijiki seaweed, and the white and black beans. Others are more concentrated sources of energy and higher in fat (see Table 1.4). Calcium-fortified soy milk can be used in rice pudding or as a beverage. Sesame tahini contributes creaminess and calcium to sauces and soups.

Soy- and rice-based beverages that are not fortified with calcium are not part of this food group and should not be relied on as calcium sources. Although the specific beans and greens listed above are good sources of calcium, others are not. Kidney beans, for example, are low in calcium. Spinach and chard contain calcium but it is not bio-available, as the calcium present is permanently locked into a complex with a substance called oxalate.

Beans & Alternatives: for protein, iron and zinc

The foods in this group are notable for their contributions of trace minerals, B vitamins and protein. As you can see in Table 1.3, all the food groups contribute protein to our diets. Legumes (beans, peas and lentils) tend to be a little more concentrated as protein sources, with 21 to 30% of their calories derived from protein. The pattern of amino acids in legumes, and especially in tofu and other soy foods, tends to be very well suited to human needs. The abundance and quality of protein in legumes make them especially valuable for growing children and for others who have increased protein needs.

When we omit meat from the diet, the initial response of many people is "Where will you get your protein?" A more apt response would be "Where will you get your saturated fat and cholesterol?" Like all plant foods, beans are cholesterol free. Most beans, with the exception of soybeans, are very low in fat.

The Beans & Alternatives food group is a primary provider of iron, significant in the prevention of anemia. This food group also features zinc, a mineral with many important roles to play in the immune system, growth and sexual development and function. An adequate intake of zinc is essential at any age, particularly during pregnancy and during the growing years from infancy through adolescence.

Omega-3 fatty acid sources

Certain components of oils, known as the omega-6 and omega-3 fatty acids, are essential to life. They perform necessary roles transporting substances in and out of cells and in health maintenance. The essential fatty acid in the omega-6 family is fairly easy to come by and is present in such a wide range of plant foods that an insufficiency is unlikely. However, substantial amounts of omega-3 fatty acids are present in fewer foods and are vulnerable to destruction by heat, light and oxygen. Because of this, we have made a point of including dietary sources of omega-3 fatty acids in many of the recipes. One of the easiest ways to get omega-3 is from flaxseed oil, used in a salad dressing or drizzled on cooked vegetables or grains. Other excellent sources are unrefined canola or soybean oils, a handful of walnuts, or a portion of firm tofu. Leafy greens contain small amounts of omega-3 fatty acids.

Vitamin B12

Ensure a source (food or supplement) supplying 1 microgram (μg) vitamin B12 daily, and 3 μg during pregnancy and lactation. Sources for vegetarians that supply 1 μg vitamin B12 are:

> Vegetarian Support Formula Nutritional Yeast (Red Star T6635+), 1 tsp (5 mL) powder or 2 tsp (10 mL) flakes (used in many of our recipes)
>
> Fortified food supplying 1 μg vitamin B12 (also listed on the label as cobalamin)
>
> 1 large egg
>
> 1 1/4 cups (300 mL) milk (whole, 2% or skim)
>
> 1 1/4 cups (300 mL) yogurt
>
> 5 oz (150 g) cheese
>
> Vitamin supplements (see label)

Vitamin D

We can produce our own vitamin D when we have adequate exposure to sunlight (ultraviolet radiation) on our hands and face. It doesn't take a lot of sun to get our daily quota – 10 to 15 minutes of sun for light-skinned people, and 1/2 hour or more for dark-skinned people. In the more populated parts of Canada, adults generally store enough vitamin D to last them through the winter, whereas young children will need a fortified food or supplement.

Balance in protein, fat and carbohydrate

Nutritional guidelines beyond those given in food guides have been developed to further help people in adopting healthful eating patterns. One such guideline addresses the distribution of the calories in our overall diet among the three nutrients that contribute calories: protein, fat and carbohydrate. Extensive scientific research has clearly indicated a connection between over-consumption of dietary fat and the chronic diseases common to the affluent countries of the world. For a longer, healthier life, a shift away from animal fats and toward the complex carbohydrates found in plant foods is advised. This dietary shift has been linked with a decreased incidence of coronary heart disease, various cancers, hypertension, strokes, bowel disorders and other chronic diseases.

Current intakes of fat in Canada and the United States are, on average, 33 to 38% of total calories. To our credit, fat intake has been slowly but steadily dropping in response to national health directives. In a 1991 technical report, the World Health Organization recommended that adults receive between 15 and 30% of the total calories in their diet from fats (Table 1.1). They added that the upper limit of 30% should be considered an interim goal and that further health benefits could be expected if fat intake is further reduced, toward the lower end of this range. Table 1.2 shows some of the foods contributing to high levels of dietary fat in the Canadian diet. Table 1.3 presents caloric distributions of selected foods in the Vegetarian Food Guide. Compare the distribution of calories among protein, fat and carbohydrate recommended by the World Health Organization (Table 1.1) with the distributions in any of the foods in Tables 1.2 and 1.3.

We are encouraged to moderate our intakes of fat and animal protein and to increase complex carbohydrate and fiber in our diets. Fiber, present only in plant food, plays a major role in maintaining bowel health and is a valuable part of the defence against other chronic diseases. As you can see from these tables, current dietary recommendations translate easily into a diet centered on plant foods.

TABLE 1.1

Distribution in diet recommended by World Health Organization*

% calories from:	Protein	Fat	Carbohydrate
	10–15	15–30	55–75

*World Health Organization Study Group on Diet, Nutrition and Prevention of Non-communicable Diseases. Geneva, Switzerland, Technical Report Series No. 797. 1991.

TABLE 1.2

Distribution of calories from protein, fat and carbohydrate, in selected foods in the standard Canadian diet

% calories from:	Protein	Fat	Carbohydrate
Mayonnaise	1	98	1
Low-cal mayonnaise	0	79	21
Potato chips	5	59	36
French fries	5	46	49
Regular beef patty, broiled	34	66	0
Lean beef patty, broiled	48	52	0
Chicken thigh, roasted, skinless	51	49	0
Sockeye salmon	53	47	0
Cheddar cheese	25	74	1
Parmesan cheese	37	60	3
Part-skim mozzarella cheese	39	57	4
Grilled cheese sandwich	18	51	31
Sugars	0	0	100
Oils, margarine and butter	0	100	0

Different needs

The tables in this chapter are here to help you make dietary choices, depending on your particular needs. Within each food group in the Vegetarian Food Guide are both high-fat and low-fat selections, as shown in Table 1.4.

Many people will find to their delight that an emphasis on grains, vegetables, fruits and the lower-fat legumes will cause them to shed

TABLE 1.3

Distribution of calories from protein, fat and carbohydrate, by food group

% calories from:	Protein	Fat	Carbohydrate
GRAINS	9–17	5–16	67–82
VEGETABLES	8–40	1–11	49–91
FRUITS	1–8	1–5	91–94
MILK & ALTERNATIVES			
Tofu, firm made with calcium	40	49	11
White, navy, great northern & black turtle beans	24–27	2–4	69–73
Almonds, sesame butters	11–14	74–76	13
Broccoli, kale, Chinese cabbage, bok choy	23–36	9–11	53–67
2% milk*	27	35	38
Assorted cheeses	25–39	57–74	1–4
BEANS & ALTERNATIVES			
Peas, lentils & most beans	21–30	1–3	67–71
Garbanzo beans (chick-peas)	21	14	65
Light silken tofu	61	27	12
Textured soy protein	60	3	37
Nuts & seeds	11–14	74–76	13
Eggs	35	62	3

*This milk is 2% fat by weight but more than one-third (38%) of its calories come from fat. The carbohydrate present is lactose, the sugar associated with lactose intolerance.

unwanted pounds. To keep those pounds off, only occasionally choose foods from the High-Calorie, High-Fat column on the right in the table on the next page and eat more of the Low-Calorie, Low-Fat foods. Note that vegetarian diets with a heavy reliance on grilled cheese sandwiches, other high-fat dairy products and eggs can still be high in saturated fat and cholesterol.

Adults who are a little leaner than they want to be, athletes who burn a tremendous number of calories, and active hungry children and teens can eat more of the High-Calorie, High-Fat options from the chart below. Although the recommendations for 15 to 30% of calories from fat apply to adults, young children thrive on a somewhat higher proportion of fat and benefit from the regular inclusion of foods such as tofu and nut butters.

TABLE 1.4

Low-Calorie, Low-Fat and High-Calorie, High-Fat choices in each food group

Food Group	Low-Calorie, Low-Fat	High-Calorie, High-Fat
GRAINS *Energy foods*	All grains and pastas are low in fat.	Some grain products are high in fat, such as many crackers, muffins and croissants.
VEGETABLES & FRUITS *Protective foods*	Almost all vegetables are low fat. Fruits and juices	Avocados, olives
MILK & ALTERNATIVES *Calcium-rich foods*	Broccoli, kale, Chinese cabbage, bok choy, light tofu made with calcium, seaweed, low-fat calcium-fortified soy milk, skim milk	Almonds, sesame seeds and their butters, tofu made with calcium, regular calcium-fortified soy milk, cheeses, whole milk
BEANS & ALTERNATIVES *Protein, iron and zinc foods*	Peas, lentils & most beans, low-fat meat substitutes or analogues, textured soy protein (TVP), low-fat soy milk	Soybeans, tofu, regular soy milk, peanuts, nuts, seeds, nut & seed butters, eggs

About the Nutritional Analysis beside each recipe

For recipes listing alternative ingredients, analysis was done using the first ingredient listed and the lesser quantity where there is a range. Unless otherwise specified, optional ingredients are not included in the analysis. Nutrient values greater than 0.4 have been rounded to the nearest whole number. A rating system provides information on the presence of selected minerals, vitamins and omega-3 fatty acids, comparing the amounts in one serving with a standard used in food labeling known as the RDI (Recommended Daily Intake).

> Where a serving provides greater than (>)25% of RDI, it is listed as an *excellent source*

> Where a serving provides 15-24% of RDI, it is listed as a *good source*

> Where a serving provides 5-14% of RDI, it is listed as a *source*

TABLE 1.5

RDI Rating System

Nutrient	RDI Standard	Excellent Source	Good Source	Source
Calcium	1100 mg	>275 mg	165–274 mg	55–164 mg
Iron	13 mg	>3.25 mg	1.95–3.25 mg	0.65–1.94 mg
Magnesium	250 mg	>62 mg	38–61 mg	12–37 mg
Zinc	12 mg	>3.0 mg	1.8–2.9 mg	0.6–1.7 mg
Folate	230 µg	>58 µg	34–57 µg	12–33 µg
Niacin	23 mg	>5.8 mg	3.4–5.7 mg	1.2–3.3 mg
Riboflavin	1.6 mg	>0.4 mg	0.24–0.39 mg	0.8–0.23 mg
Thiamin	1.3 mg	>0.32 mg	0.2–0.31 mg	0.06–0.19 mg
Vitamin A	1000 RE*	>250 RE	150–249 RE	50–149 RE
Vitamin B12	1.0 µg	>0.25 µg	0.15–0.24 µg	0.05–0.14 µg
Vitamin E	10 mg	>2.5 mg	1.5–2.4 mg	0.5–1.4 mg
Omega-3 fatty acids	1.8 g	>0.45 g	>0.27–0.44 g	0.09–0.26 g

*Retinol Equivalents

For each nutrient included in the analysis, the RDI and the range for each of these three categories is shown in Table 1.5.

Since the RDI is based on the recommended intake for the age and gender that has the highest requirements, your own recommended intake may be substantially lower. For example, recommended intakes of calcium are particularly high (1100 mg) during early adolescence, when bone growth is at its peak. In contrast, the intake recommended for adult premenopausal women is 700 mg. (If you would like to look up recommended intakes for males or females of other ages, see *Becoming Vegetarian*, page 256). The RDI is listed as 1100 mg, based on the highest recommended intake.

FIBER, SODIUM AND OTHER NUTRIENTS

It is recommended that the average daily fiber intake of an individual be 20 to 40 g. For healthy individuals, many experts recommend that sodium intake be between 500 mg and 2400 mg per day, on average. The RDI for vitamin C is 40 mg. Foods providing >20 mg are listed as excellent sources of vitamin C.

Percent Calories from Protein, Fat and Carbohydrate

The ranges of calories from protein, fat and carbohydrate recommended for adults in the overall diet are summarized in Table 1.1. Because 1 g of protein or carbohydrate each provide 4 calories whereas 1 g of fat provides 9 calories, a mere teaspoon of oil (containing 5 g of fat) added to each serving can have a substantial input on the percentage of total calories contributed by fat.

Chapter 1 provides a scientific overview for understanding the balance of foods necessary to build and maintain optimum health through a plant-based diet. Like a compass in the hands of a pioneer, the Vegetarian Food Guide is meant to be a reference, illustrating the number of servings recommended for obtaining maximum benefit from specific food groups. Once you've understood the characteristics of the food groups, you can take action and apply this knowledge to your daily life. Chapter 2 focuses on this action, so that your experience with the recipes brings you the utmost joy and well-being.

References for nutrient analysis:

Consumer and Corporate Affairs Canada, Consumer Products Branch, Food Division. *Nutrition Labelling Handbook.* 1992

The Food Processor for Windows, Quality Nutrition Analysis Software and Databases, ESHA Research, 1995. [Nutritional analysis program used for recipe analysis. 1-800-659-3742.]

Canadian Nutrient File. Pennington, Jean A.T. *Bowes & Church's Food Values of Portions Commonly Used.* 16th ed. Philadelphia: Lippincott. 1994.

United States Department of Agriculture, Agriculture Research Service. *Agricultural Handbook No 8.*

CHAPTER TWO

NOTES FROM CHEF JOSEPH

Drawing together individual food items to create a recipe is similar to a conductor bringing together the sound of individual instruments to create a symphony. The results can be spectacular and the rewards enduring. You are the conductor of your own kitchen symphony.

Food as passion

Food is the great passion of my life. As far back as I can remember, all of my senses have been curious about the endless nuances surrounding food. Food is my doorway into the world of alchemy: colors brighten, textures soften and shapes emerge and disappear before my eyes and in my hands as I marry one food to another. Under the influence and purposeful direction of fire, air and water, earth is transformed from humble origins into celebrated wholeness. This process not only nourishes my life – it is my life.

Not everyone has this kind of relationship with food. There are some who believe that eating is a chore, an interruption from a more important task. Others consider themselves inept in the kitchen and consequently fling the most basic ingredients together meal after meal. For still others, preparing meals can be a daunting experience resulting in chaos. These situations can lead to nutritionally inadequate eating patterns.

This chapter was written to help you integrate the elements that lead into and include food preparation. One of these elements is the nutritional adequacy and balance between food groups of your eating pattern as a whole. Choice of good quality ingredients is another important component. Strong organizational skills in the kitchen could be included in this mix as well as the actual preparation, cooking and presentation of food. All these are ingredients in a recipe for health. Time and attention given to these elements and how they are assembled under your guidance will have a significant impact on the quality of your life.

A central theme in cooking is choice; numerous choices present themselves every day. What shall I eat tonight? Are higher quality items worth the extra expense? What method of cooking should I use? How much time do I have to cook? These are choices that need to be made according to your schedule, tastes and preferences and they will be addressed here in the hope that cooking will become and continue to be a source of great enjoyment.

These recipes have been created with health in mind, yet we all know that unless flavor is present it doesn't matter how healthy food is. Our approach is to use food, herbs and spices that are fresh and in as natural a state as possible to create great-tasting food. Furthermore, we encourage you to use the recipes as a guideline, to work with them, adjust them and tailor them to your own particular tastes.

A distinct feature in many of these recipes is 'oil-free sautéing' for those who wish to reduce the amount of oil in their diet. This cooking technique is straightforward and does not require any extra time. Those who believe that the use of oil is critical to cooking may want to try the oil-free option on occasion.

Choices in the market place

The market is brimming with variety. Food stores offer every conceivable product in myriad shapes, sizes and colors. Grocery departments feature produce from every part of the world and trade names and food brands compete for your attention and loyalty at each turn. All these possibilities add up to a mountain of decisions and can be confusing. A knowledge of our Vegetarian Food Guide, coupled with discernment, are useful tools in navigating through this land of a thousand choices. To help narrow down your decisions, consider these two recommended food categories:

1. Those that retain their natural complement of nutrients
2. Those that are organically grown

Foods that retain their natural complement of nutrients

Nature packages food in perfect ways that we have yet to improve upon. In plants, bundles of energy in complex carbohydrates, building properties in protein, and health-protective essential fatty acids in oils are combined in amounts that are exquisitely balanced. When foods are whole, or close to their natural states, elements such as vitamins and phytochemicals provide natural defenses against deterioration. For example, when a walnut is in its shell, protective membranes surround the meat of the nut, and vitamin E and other antioxidants in the nut oils protect valuable omega-3 fatty acids from oxidation and rancidity. After months on a store shelf, shelled walnuts have lost much of their flavor and the health-supportive properties they impart to us. For a fresh product, shell nuts just before use or choose shelled walnuts from a store that has a high turnover or keeps nuts refrigerated.

Foods such as fruits, vegetables, unrefined cereal grains, legumes, nuts and seeds can be found in the marketplace with little change from their state in the farmer's field. Such foods have high nutritional density, that is, they provide plenty of nutritional value per calorie of food energy. They are also richer in natural flavors, and do not need artificial flavor enhancers. It makes sense to center your diet on foods chosen from this group.

Don't imagine that the choice of healthy eating requires that you spend long hours in the kitchen preparing foods from scratch. With the growing appetite of consumers for healthful foods, more ingredients are available that have been processed to make them easy to use, at the same time retaining top nutritional quality. Examples are tofu, nut and seed butters and whole grain pastas. Our recipes are full of such ingredients. Spend a little time browsing the aisles or freezer of a local health food store or natural foods section of a major supermarket. You'll discover many new nutrition-packed products. Many of these products didn't exist even a few years ago, and the flavor and quality have come a long way in our competitive marketplace. Another area of growth is convenience foods. Deli counters offer a wonderful array of prepared foods. Consider buying one or two tasty side dishes at a deli to accompany a quickly prepared salad and cooked grain.

Organic foods

Organic agriculture is a system of farming that uses a variety of safe and environmentally friendly practices to grow food. Some of these methods include natural pest control, crop rotation, composting, mulching and the use of pest-resistant seed varieties. The purpose is to create a fertile environment for plants as well as birds, predatory insects, earthworms, and microorganisms. The result is soil that is rich and arable. Organic food is gaining popularity due to its positive effect on human health and the world's soil, fresh water supply and atmosphere. Choosing food for its health-supporting properties could include a choice that sustains the planet Earth. A thought to consider is that every time you buy organic products you are making a powerful vote for a healthier world to live in.

The transition to organic

Choosing to put organic food on your table can be as significant and gradual a change as opting for a vegetarian diet. You don't have to convert your refrigerator or your pantry overnight. As you become familiar with organic foods, you'll discover that their availability is increasing. Produce departments of large food stores are beginning to offer a variety of organic food products as their managers discover positive customer response. Farmer's markets, natural food stores and co-ops carry a wide selection of organic produce.

Choose the best quality ingredients your budget allows

Since nutrients are a big factor in supporting health, it makes sense to purchase ingredients that give you the biggest nutritional return for your dollar. The cost of outfitting your kitchen with healthy food might appear expensive, yet the cost often proves worthwhile in the long run. Perhaps you can learn from one of my own experiences. When I used to purchase pure olive oil for use in Hummus, I would use 1/4 cup of oil to satisfy my taste. Since I have discovered extra-virgin olive oil, I've reduced to 1 tablespoon the amount of oil I now use for the same dish, because it has such flavor. (Olives are pressed several times to extract every possible drop of oil. The first pressings, which are the most flavorful, are "extra virgin-olive oil". The last pressings, labeled "pure olive oil", are not as flavorful.) At first the oil appears to cost more; however, I get better mileage from the higher-quality oil, since I use much less.

As you become familiar with the qualities and health benefits of various ingredients, you will be in a better position to make wise decisions. Ask questions about products and read labels. Trust your tastes. Remember, this is your journey. Make a choice and if it's not the best one for you, make another choice. In time you will become more confident in the use of a variety of new kitchen staples.

Organization as the key to your success

Once your shopping has yielded ingredients to take home, the next step is preparing all the goodies you've bought. This is where the system breaks down for many people. The manner in which you approach your food preparation can make or break your cooking enjoyment. The key to success is organization.

During my chef's training, the emphasis was on preparing for the pressures and unexpected requests that bombard a professional kitchen during peak service times. A lot of time was devoted to organization. The French term for this is *mise en place*, meaning "everything in its place." We developed this skill so that minimal time was spent running around the kitchen once service began.

Like a busy professional chef, you have your own deadlines, pressures, unexpected interruptions and last-minute requests. You may not have as much time to spend in the kitchen as you would like; however, some rudimentary organizational skills can maximize your productivity and efficiency. The following steps can help you have a more enjoyable experience in the kitchen.

1. READ YOUR RECIPE FIRST

Develop the habit of reading your chosen recipes from beginning to end. This gives you an overview of the foods, techniques and equipment required. It also stimulates your thinking about the task at hand and how you are going to accomplish it.

2. GATHER ALL EQUIPMENT NEEDED

This includes cutting board, knives, mixing bowls, measuring cups, spoons, food processor and pots. This step may prompt you to read the recipe again, which is the real key to the exercise. Reading the recipe a second time further deepens your understanding of what you are about to perform. The clearer your idea of what you are about to do, the less chaos there will be at the kitchen counter or stove.

3. GATHER ALL THE INGREDIENTS

Knowing up front that you have all your ingredients eliminates the frustration of discovering half way through a recipe that you didn't stock up on an important staple. Gathering everything at the beginning requires less time than if you periodically interrupt your cutting or measuring to return to the refrigerator for an additional ingredient.

While you are preparing ingredients for the recipe, this is the time when the oven could be pre-heating, water could be on to boil for pasta, or the soup pot could be pre-warming at the lowest setting.

4. SET UP YOUR COUNTER SPACE

This is not so much a step as a pattern to follow each time you prepare food. How you arrange and organize your ingredients and equipment determines how smoothly the final product comes into being. My approach to how I prepare the Szechuan Vegetables over Buckwheat Noodles (page 132) might serve as an example.

All my kitchen utensils are already assembled in a wicker basket to the left of the stove. I lay a damp dishcloth flat on the counter and set my cutting board on top to prevent slipping – a valuable safety tip when using sharp knives. My skillet is pre-heating on the lowest heat setting. I place the washed ingredients that need to be prepped on the left side of the cutting board. As vegetables are cut they are placed in separate piles on a large plate to the right of the board. All herbs and spices are measured into a small bowl, wet ingredients into a second bowl. Ingredients no longer needed are placed out of the way and I now proceed to the stove where I am poised to cook.

How you set up your counter space is partly determined by how much space you have to work with. If you are short of counter space, perhaps a portable table such as a TV tray could be brought into the kitchen when needed, to help in organizing your ingredients.

When all ingredients are prepped and gathered within arm's reach, the actual cooking of food becomes a much easier task, whether you are making a stir-fry or assembling sushi. You won't have to worry about burning the onions while you're still cutting carrots. Your counter space will be much clearer, thus your kitchen won't look as if Hurricane Andrew just passed through. Developing this habit can go a long way toward alleviating kitchen chaos.

The use of oil in cooking

Many people believe that oil is crucial to cooking and that without its liberal use, cooking is not possible. Vegetable oil in cooking and baking does serve several purposes. Perhaps the most obvious one is that it prevents food from sticking to the pan, pot or barbecue grill. Oil is an excellent conductor of heat, so when foods are coated with oil at high temperatures as in a stir-fry, they cook very rapidly. Vegetable oil and fat add moisture to food and consequently increase the shelf life or quality of products like bread, cakes and cookies. Adding oil to food also gives it smoothness and a pleasant "mouth feel", as it does with Hummus. Perhaps the most common feature of oil is its ability to act as a carrier for flavor, as evident in salad dressings. Overall, consumption of oil is high in our national diet, but this is changing as the evidence builds linking high fat and oil intake to a decline in health.

No-oil cooking as an option

Although certain components of oils are an essential part of good nutrition, for most North Americans, fats provide far too large a proportion of total calories. Realizing this, a growing number of people with health and weight problems are cutting back on their use of fats and oils. Those looking for ways to reduce the calories from fat in their diet have found that, instead of sautéing food in oil, they can sauté with vegetable stock or water. Many of the recipes in this book feature this liquid sautéing method; however, we also provide the option of using oil. The analysis below these recipes includes nutrient figures for both methods. You may want to compare the distribution of calories without oil and with oil with the recommended caloric distribution in Table 1.1 on page 12. You may want to use the oil-free cooking method exclusively, on occasion or not at all.

Whether you use vegetable stock, water or oil for sautéing food, the goal is the same: to develop flavor and bring out the sweetness of the vegetables. As the sautéing liquid evaporates, the sugars in the vegetables caramelize and add sweetness. Sautéing in too much liquid results in boiling, which does not provide the sweetness of caramelization.

The technique for oil-free sautéing is as follows. Sauté the vegetables over medium high heat in 2 tbsp (30 mL) of vegetable stock or water to start, adding 1-2 tbsp (15-30 mL) more stock if necessary. To control the rate of evaporation and to keep it to a minimum, use a lid or lower the cooking temperature. Use stock whenever possible as this adds more flavor than water. A number of vegetable stock powders, cubes and canned stocks are available on the market, but our recommendation is to avoid products that contain hydrogenated oil. If you want to try making your own stock for more control over the final taste, see page 101. Once you familiarize yourself with this cooking method, keeping a jar of stock on hand in the refrigerator makes sense. You may want to double or triple the recipe and freeze some for up to 3 months. Ice cube trays will hold 2 tbsp (30 mL) of liquid per cube, which is the amount of liquid that will be called for in most recipes. When the cubes are frozen, remove them from the tray and store them in a freezer bag. Make more, so you always have stock cubes on hand.

Unrefined oils for flavor

If one of the functions of oil is to provide flavor, does reducing oil in the diet mean less-flavorful food? The answer is no. The cooking oils that we suggest you eliminate or reduce in the diet are highly refined commercial oils. Modern oil production subjects seeds and their oils to many processes including hexane solvent extraction, degumming, bleaching and deodorizing. Temperatures reach from 130°F to over 500°F for periods of 30 to 60 minutes. The resulting oil is devoid of many nutritional qualities that were initially present in the seed. The oils recommended for use in this book are unrefined. Although they too have been crushed, pressing temperatures, particularly for flaxseed oil, range between 86° and 92°F. Oils pressed at lower temperatures retain important nutritional elements. Also, these oils carry the flavor of the seed or nut from which they were pressed. For example, extra-virgin olive oil tastes like olives and unrefined sunflower oil tastes like sunflower seeds. Unrefined oils can be used in salad dressings, as a last-minute garnish for soup, and over rice, noodles and steamed vegetables. Flaxseed oil may even be used on hot breakfast cereal or in the Fruit Shake, page 36.

Aromatic oils in herbs and spices for developing flavor

Herbs are aromatic plants used for seasoning food or medicinal purposes. Culinary herbs such as bay, basil, oregano, thyme, parsley and sage are often grown in temperate climates and their leaves are the part of the plant used in cooking. Spices, on the other hand, are aromatic plants that are generally pungent and originate from tropical lands. The plant parts generally used are roots (ginger), bark (cinnamon), flowers (saffron), berries (allspice and pepper), seeds (cumin and caraway), pods (vanilla and cardamom) and fruit (anise seed and tamarind).

In any cuisine, herbs and spices draw upon the powerful aromatic oils contained in a plant. These oils have distinctive aromas, ranging from subtle to intense, and when released into the food they impart specific tastes and fragrances. What also makes these oils attractive is their distinctive health supportive properties. For instance, cumin, fennel and ginger added to food all promote digestion. When consistently used in your diet, they can be advantageous to your health over time.

Since aromatic oils are very volatile, they begin dispersing into the atmosphere immediately upon harvesting. Consequently, fresh herbs are better to use than dried. The roots, barks, whole seeds and berries of spices are hardier and will retain their oils longer than the delicate leaves of herbs. However, once ground into powder, they quickly lose their potency.

Herbs and spices are best purchased from a store where there is a high turnover of these staples. They keep best when stored in airtight containers in the dark space of a closed cupboard. Dark glass or opaque jars with tight-fitting lids are a good investment to keep damaging light out and precious oils in. Avoid storing your herbs and spices near the warm environment of a stove as the valuable oils will quickly dissipate, making them less effective. Dried herbs should be replaced within six months, spices within one year.

Adjust the seasoning

The last instruction in most recipes, whether written or assumed, is "adjust the seasoning" or "season to taste." Although this usually implies adding salt and pepper, it is an opportunity to adjust the recipe to suit your tastes and preferences with seasonings or flavorings. The ability to evaluate and correct the final flavors of a dish is a valuable skill, so take the time to be mindful at this stage.

Using the recipe as a guideline

Remember, a recipe is a set of instructions that brings together ingredients to achieve a final product. But these instructions and ingredients are not carved in stone. They are meant to act as a guide to steer you in a particular direction. We encourage you to follow a recipe once to get a sense of it, then decide if it is worth repeating. You may even want to adjust an ingredient or two before you start: for instance, tahini may not be your favorite seed or nut butter but perhaps almond butter is. Therefore, in the Happy Heart Granola recipe on page 41, you could exchange one butter for another. The concentrated apple juice in the same recipe could replace the maple syrup altogether. In a soup a different combination of vegetables or beans may be more to your taste, or maybe you would prefer rice instead of noodles. We do recommend, however, that if you try an ingredient such as tofu or flaxseed oil for the first time, and the recipe wasn't pleasing, consider giving the ingredient another chance in a different recipe.

Garnishing as the final adjustment

Before serving, take a few minutes to create an ambiance for the delicious food you have prepared. Garnishing food creates balance, harmony and beauty. A garnish has a way of uplifting the mood and spirit of the cook as well as those who will be served. On a deeper level, adding a final touch to the meal can be a tremendous act of respect and love, for you, your family and the food. Simply stated, garnishing is an art form that has the power to nourish the soul.

Garnishes do not have to be as complicated as carving flowers out of carrots or forming a rose bud from the long unbroken peeled skin of a tomato. A garnish should contrast with the main colors of the food and be applied in odd numbers. For example, if olives are your garnish on top of a salad or platter, use 1, 3, or 5 rather than 2, 4, or 6. Ideas for garnishing your food include chopped or whole leaves of fresh herbs, wedges of lemon or tomato, or capers. Finely diced red, yellow or orange sweet peppers, finely chopped green onion, sprouts, grated radish, carrot or zucchini all have their place in adding a final touch to the meal. When sprinkling powders such as paprika, place a bit in the palm of one hand and use your other hand to pinch and sprinkle.

In the past few years, the use of whole flowers or their petals in salads or on the rim of a plate has become an effective way of raising the enjoyment level of a meal. The delicate reds, blues, purples and pinks are very pleasing to the eye and can create a new dimension to an eating experience. Be cautious when picking your own flowers by making certain they are edible and haven't been sprayed.

Nourishing properties of beauty

The beauty reflected in the garnish of your plate can be extended to your table. In my own home I arrange fresh cut flowers in a vase and light candles. Eating is a time when I open up to receive more than just nourishment from food. Good company, conversation, music, laughter and the beauty found at home are nourishing components to my meal that are just as significant as the food I have chosen for its wholesome content. Mirth and joy garnishes my table as much as the flowers do. Above all, meal times are a time of rest, a place where I truly find comfort in the gifts of the earth.

May your body, mind and soul be truly nourished.

MENU SELECTIONS

The combination of recipes found in the following menu selections, reflect a blending of ingredients, flavors, seasonings and colors that are common in many homes around the world. Choose a few for a simple meal, or more for a larger gathering or an evening of entertaining. The selections range from the everyday fast and easy dishes as found in the Canadian Selections to more complex choices for festive times from the Thanksgiving and Christmas Selections.

Canadian Menu Selections

Gee Whiz Spread on Crackers   *52*

Vegetable Noodle Soup   *100*

Sliced Tomatoes with Cucumber Dill Dressing   *80*

Open Faced Tofu Sandwich   *121*

Potato Wedges with Dipping Sauces   *152*

Pumpkin Pie with Holiday Pie Topping   *185, 190*

Chinese Menu Selections

Fresh Vegetable Salad Roll with Peanut Sauce   *70, 164*

Mushroom Broth   *97*

Calcium-Rich Greens   *66*

Oriental Dressing   *85*

Sweet and Sour Tofu   *131*

Bok Choy, Mushrooms and Ginger   *140*

Green Beans with Black Beans   *145*

Brown Rice Pudding   *180*

Lemon Sesame Cookies   *186*

French Menu Selections

Indian Menu Selections

Italian Menu Selections

Japanese Menu Selections

Beverages
& Breakfasts

ALMOND MILK

Although almonds and other nuts are high in fat, they are also rich in trace minerals. For a concentrated source of energy, use this nut milk as a beverage, on cereal or in a fruit shake. Since some of the calcium is in the pulp, if you strain it, you may want to add the pulp to baking, cereals, soups, gravy, sauces or rice.

PER 1-CUP (250 ML)
SERVING

calories 191
protein 7 g
fat 17 g
carbohydrate 7 g
dietary fiber 3 g
sodium 11 mg

Excellent source of:
magnesium
Good source of:
riboflavin
Source of:
calcium, iron, zinc,
folate, niacin, thiamin,
omega-3 fatty acids

% Calories from:
protein 13%
fat 74%
carbohydrate 13%

2 cups	water	500 mL
1/2 cup	shelled blanched almonds	125 mL
1 tbsp	maple syrup or other sweetener (optional)	15 mL

Put water, almonds and maple syrup (if using) into blender and process on high speed for 1 minute or until smooth. Can be stored in refrigerator for 4 to 5 days. Shake before using.

Makes 2-1/4 cups (550 mL) with pulp.

FESTIVE HOLIDAY PUNCH

Fresh gingerroot makes a rich taste contribution to this punch and adds a tiny nip to the tongue. Simmering the ginger briefly in water releases its flavor, which is then incorporated with the sweetness of the fruit juices.

1-1/2 cups	water	375 mL
1 cup	Sucanat or brown sugar	250 mL
3 tbsp	peeled, chopped gingerroot	45 mL
4	whole cloves	4
1/2 tsp	ground cinnamon	2 mL
1/4 tsp	ground nutmeg	1 mL
3 cups	orange juice	750 mL
3 cups	apple juice	750 mL
3 cups	cranberry juice	750 mL
1	orange, sliced thinly	1

In covered pot, bring to boil water, Sucanat, gingerroot, cloves, cinnamon and nutmeg. Reduce heat, cover and simmer 5 minutes. Let steep 1 hour. Combine orange, apple and cranberry juices in large jar or container. Strain ginger concentrate into fruit juices, cover and refrigerate 4 hours. Pour into punch bowl and garnish with orange slices.

Makes 12 servings, each 1 cup (250 mL)

PER SERVING

calories 144
protein 1 g
fat 0.2 g
carbohydrate 36 g
dietary fiber 0.5 g
sodium 10 mg

Excellent source of:
vitamin C
Source of:
iron, magnesium, manganese, potassium, folate, thiamin, vitamin B6

% Calories from:
protein 2%
fat 1%
carbohydrate 97%

Sucanat (*sugar cane natural*) is a tasty golden brown granular sugar derived from organic cane juice, with the water removed but retaining trace minerals found naturally in the sugar cane plant. It may be used as a more nutritious one-for-one replacement for white refined or brown sugar.

FRUIT SHAKES

These shakes are favorites as quick breakfasts, after-school snacks, a boost for athletes and nutritious beverages for seniors. Ripe bananas give the sweetest flavor. You may also replace the fruits used below with seasonal fruits.

STRAWBERRY SHAKE

I	pkg (10 oz/300 g) soft tofu	I
1-1/2 cups	frozen strawberries, thawed	375 mL
I	ripe banana	I
3/4 cup	water	175 mL

Place tofu, strawberries, banana and water in blender or food processor and blend until smooth.

ORANGE SHAKE

I	pkg (10 oz/300 g) soft tofu	I
1 cup	frozen orange juice concentrate	250 mL
I	ripe banana	I
1-1/2 cups	water	375 mL

Place tofu, juice, banana and water in blender or food processor and blend until smooth.

Makes 4 servings, each 1 cup (250 mL)

PER SERVING
STRAWBERRY SHAKE

calories 82
protein 4 g
fat 3 g
carbohydrate 12 g
dietary fiber 2 g
sodium 7 mg

Excellent source of:
vitamin C
Source of:
iron, magnesium,
folate, riboflavin,
thiamin, vitamin E

% Calories from:
protein 19%
fat 26%
carbohydrate 55%

PER SERVING
ORANGE SHAKE

calories 179
protein 6 g
fat 3 g
carbohydrate 36 g
dietary fiber 1 g
sodium 10 mg

Excellent source of:
folate, vitamin C
Good source of:
magnesium, thiamin
Source of:
iron, zinc, riboflavin,
vitamin E

% Calories from:
protein 12%
fat 12%
carbohydrate 76%

HOT APPLE CIDER

The inviting aromas of spices fill the air while this warming drink simmers on the stove. It will delight people of all ages after a skating party or autumn walk or taken along on a winter outing.

2 cups	apple juice	500 mL
1/4 tsp	each ground cinnamon and nutmeg	1 mL
1/8 tsp	each ground cloves and allspice	0.5 mL
2 cups	cranberry juice	500 mL

In small jar with lid, combine cinnamon, nutmeg, cloves and allspice with 1/4 cup of the apple juice. Close lid and shake vigorously until blended. Pour into pot and add remaining apple juice and cranberry juice. Heat just to boiling.

Makes 4 servings, each 1 cup (250 mL)

PER SERVING

calories 132
protein 0.1 g
fat 0.3 g
carbohydrate 33 g
dietary fiber 0.4 g
sodium 7 mg

Excellent source of:
vitamin C
Source of:
iron

% Calories from:
protein 1%
fat 2%
carbohydrate 97%

SOY MILK CAPPUCCINO

Inspired by a beverage served by Robert-Michael Kaplan, author of *Seeing Without Glasses*, this is a healthy, delicious alternative to the '90s café choice. Experiment with different coffee substitutes or cocoa, then cozy up with a good book on a cool night.

PER SERVING

calories 113
protein 7 g
fat 4 g
carbohydrate 13 g
dietary fiber 3 g
sodium 30 mg

Good source of:
magnesium, thiamin
(and calcium if using
calcium-fortified
soy milk)
Source of:
iron, zinc

% Calories from:
protein 21%
fat 33%
carbohydrate 46%

1 cup	soy milk, unflavored	250 mL
2 tsp	maple syrup, brown sugar or honey	10 mL
2 tsp	grain beverage powder (Pero, Caf Lib) or unsweetened cocoa powder	10 mL
1/4 tsp	vanilla extract	1 mL
Pinch	ground cinnamon	Pinch
	Chocolate shavings (optional)	

Heat soy milk until just below boiling in saucepan over medium high heat or in microwave at High for 2 minutes. Remove from heat. Stir in maple syrup, grain beverage powder, vanilla and cinnamon and beat with egg beater until frothy. Pour into mug and garnish with chocolate shavings (if using).

Makes one 1-cup (250 mL) serving

APPLE MUESLI

You'll look forward to breakfast, with this make-ahead combination waiting for you. Prepared the night before, it makes a nourishing instant breakfast for one hungry person, or can be divided between two. Many people like to eat this for dessert or as an evening snack. If you prefer it less sweet, use a combination of apple juice and water. For variations, add grated apple or mashed ripe banana just before serving.

1-1/4 cups	apple juice	300 mL
1 cup	rolled oats	250 mL
2 tbsp	raisins or currants, chopped dates or nuts	30 mL
1/8 tsp	ground cinnamon	0.5 mL
Pinch	of any 2 of ground nutmeg, coriander, allspice or cloves	Pinch

In bowl, combine apple juice, rolled oats, raisins, cinnamon and the 2 spices of your choice. Mix, cover and refrigerate 2 hours or overnight.

Makes 1 large 1-1/2 cup (375 mL) serving or 2 regular servings

PER LARGE SERVING

calories 512
protein 14 g
fat 6 g
carbohydrate 105 g
dietary fiber 9 g
sodium 15 mg

Excellent source of:
iron, magnesium, zinc, thiamin
Good source of:
vitamin E
Source of:
calcium, folate, niacin, riboflavin, omega-3 fatty acids

% Calories from:
protein 10%
fat 9%
carbohydrate 81%

FRESH FRUIT SALAD

Starting the day with the tang of grapefruit and the zing of orange can be uplifting and awakening. Packed with vitamin C, fresh fruit offers protection against environmental stresses. Vary this salad with fruits of the seasons and treat yourself to organic whenever possible.

1	banana, peeled and sliced	1
1	grapefruit, peeled and sectioned	1
1	apple, chopped	1
1	pear, chopped	1
1/2 cup	orange juice	125 mL
sprig	fresh mint, chopped (optional)	sprig

Combine chopped fruit in bowl. Pour orange juice over fruit. Garnish with mint (if using).

Makes 2 servings, each serving 1-1/8 cups (275 mL)

HAPPY HEART GRANOLA

This granola can be baked in the oven on baking trays, in a roasting pan or in a large metal bowl. The results will give you a healthy, delicious and easy start to your days for a week or two. If you like, you may replace the maple syrup by an additional 1/2 cup (125 mL) apple juice concentrate.

1/2 cup	apple juice concentrate	125 mL
1/2 cup	almond butter or tahini	125 mL
1/2 cup	maple syrup	125 mL
1 tsp	vanilla or almond extract	5 mL
8 cups	rolled oats	2 L
1 cup	chopped almonds or sunflower seeds (optional)	250 mL
1 cup	raisins, currants or chopped dates	250 mL

Combine apple juice concentrate, almond butter, maple syrup and vanilla in a bowl or blender. Mix well. Combine oats and almonds (if using) in a large bowl or roasting pan. Pour liquid mixture over oats and stir to coat evenly. Spread out evenly in the roasting pan, on baking trays or up along the sides of a metal bowl. Bake in 350°F oven for 30 minutes or until golden brown, stirring every 10 minutes to prevent burning. Cool, stir in fruit and store in jar with lid or plastic bags.

Makes 11 cups (2.7 L)

PER CUP (250 mL)

calories 400
protein 12 g
fat 11 g
carbohydrate 67 g
dietary fiber 7 g
sodium 10 mg

Excellent source of:
iron, magnesium,
thiamin, vitamin E
Good source of:
zinc
Source of:
calcium, folate,
riboflavin

% Calories from:
protein 11%
fat 23%
carbohydrate 66%

OATMEAL PORRIDGE

In the age of eat-and-run, having a bowl of cooked oats can be comforting and soothing to the stomach. Flaxseed oil may sound like an unusual item to put on your hot cereal, but it's an old European tradition from the era when small opaque bottles of fresh pressed flaxseed oil were delivered to the door every week by horse and carriage. Try it, and see if you like this way of getting your omega-3s!

PER SERVING

calories 168
protein 6 g
fat 3 g
carbohydrate 31 g
dietary fiber 1 g
sodium 15 mg

Excellent source of:
iron, riboflavin,
thiamin (and omega-
3, with flaxseed oil)
Good source of:
calcium
Source of:
magnesium

Without oil:
% Calories from:
protein 13%
fat 11%
carbohydrate 77%

With oil:
protein 11%
fat 18%
carbohydrate 71%

2 cups	water	500 mL
1 cup	rolled oats	250 mL
2 tbsp	raisins or chopped dates	30 mL
1/4 tsp	ground cinnamon	1 mL
1/4 cup	soy or rice milk	60 mL
2-3 tsp	maple syrup	10-15 mL
1 tsp	flaxseed oil (optional)	5 mL

Bring water to boil in covered saucepan over high heat. Stir or whisk in rolled oats, raisins and cinnamon. Reduce heat, cover and simmer for 15 minutes (2 to 4 minutes if using quick-cooking oats), stirring occasionally. Transfer to serving bowl and garnish with milk, maple syrup and flaxseed oil (if using).

Makes 2 servings, each serving 1 cup (250 mL)

SCRAMBLED TOFU

A replacement for scrambled eggs in the morning, this no-cholesterol dish goes well with toast and juice or a hot beverage. It also makes an easy-to-assemble source of protein, vitamins and minerals at lunch or dinner time.

1 lb	medium-firm tofu	454 g
1/2 cup	sliced mushrooms	125 mL
2 tbsp	chopped green onions	30 mL
1/2	small clove garlic, minced	1/2
2 tbsp	vegetable stock or 1-1/2 tsp (7 mL) canola oil	30 mL
1 tsp	chopped fresh cilantro	5 mL
1/4 tsp	ground cumin	1 mL
1/4 tsp	salt	1 mL
Pinch	turmeric	Pinch
1 tbsp	nutritional yeast	15 mL
1 tbsp	salsa (optional)	15 mL

Press out water from tofu as described on the next page. Place tofu in bowl and mash with fork. Sauté mushrooms, green onions and garlic in vegetable stock or oil in skillet over medium heat for 3 to 5 minutes or until liquid has evaporated. Stir in tofu, cilantro, cumin, salt and turmeric; sauté for 4 to 5 minutes. Stir in yeast and salsa (if using).

Makes 2 servings

PER SERVING

calories 176
protein 19 g
carbohydrate 5 g
fat 10 g
dietary fiber 1 g
sodium 270 mg

With Oil:
calories 206
fat 13 g

Excellent source of:
calcium (using tofu made with calcium), iron, riboflavin, thiamin
Good source of:
folate, omega-3 fatty acids
Source of:
zinc, niacin

Without Oil:
% *Calories from:*
protein 41%
fat 48%
carbohydrate 11%

With Oil:
% *Calories from:*
protein 35%
fat 55%
carbohydrate 10%

DIFFERENCES IN TOFU

In the process of making tofu, hot soy milk is blended with a coagulant to form a curd. At this stage, soft tofu is poured directly into its package. For medium through extra-firm grades, the curd is poured into a mold, covered with cotton, pressed to form a block, cut and then packaged. The amount of pressure applied determines whether the tofu will be medium, firm or extra-firm in consistency. Since the textures vary for each of these types of tofu, they each have specific uses in recipes.

As blocks of tofu vary considerably, our recipes describe tofu in weight measures. When making your purchase please read the label for weight. Also look for tofu that has "calcium" on the ingredient list for a good source of dietary calcium.

Why recipes call for "pressed medium tofu"

The smoothness of the medium tofu is of value in many recipes; however, the water content may still be too high for certain recipes such as Curry Sandwich Spread, page 51, and Scrambled Tofu, page 43. If the tofu was used without first pressing out excess water, the liquid would "weep" into the bread or onto the serving plate.

How to press medium tofu

Remove tofu from package and place it on a dinner plate. Place another plate of equal size over the tofu and carefully place a 4- or 5-pound (2- to 2.2 kg) weight – e.g., 2 to 3 cans of tomato sauce – on the plate. Press the tofu for 15 to 20 minutes. At this time approximately 1/2 cup of liquid will have pooled on the bottom plate; it can be discarded. Transfer the tofu block to a bowl and proceed with the recipe.

Silken tofu

Silken tofu is particularly silky in texture. Like other tofu on the market, it ranges from soft to extra-firm. Silken tofu is poured directly into an aseptic box and needs no refrigeration before opening. Mori-Nu Silken Tofu is the most widely sold and comes in 10.5 oz (300 g) packages.

DIPS, SPREADS & SNACKS

DEBRAH'S AVOCADO DIP

Nutritional yeast packs extra punch into this creamy dip, developed by Joseph's life partner, Debrah. Serve it with rice cakes, crackers or baked tortilla chips.

PER 1/4-CUP
(60 mL) SERVING

calories 165
protein 2 g
fat 15 g
carbohydrate 8 g
dietary fiber 4 g
sodium 46 mg

Excellent source of:
folate, riboflavin,
thiamin
Good source of:
magnesium
Source of:
iron, niacin, vitamin A,
omega-3 fatty acids

% Calories from:
protein 5%
fat 77%
carbohydrate 18%

2	ripe avocados	2
2–3 tsp	lime juice	10–15 mL
1/2 tsp	tamari or soy sauce	2 mL
1 tsp	nutritional yeast	5 mL
1/4 tsp	each chili powder and garlic powder	1 mL
Pinch	pepper	Pinch
2 tsp	chopped green onions	10 mL
2 tsp	chopped fresh cilantro	10 mL

Scoop avocado flesh into bowl and mash until smooth. Blend in lime juice, tamari, yeast, chili powder, garlic powder and pepper. Stir in onions and cilantro. Adjust seasoning.

Makes 1 cup (250 mL)

BLACK BEAN HUMMUS

Keep this very low-fat dip in your refrigerator as a quick snack to serve with carrot sticks, crackers or bread. It's a great source of trace minerals and folate.

2 cups	cooked or canned black turtle beans or black beans	500 mL
2 tbsp	liquid from cooking beans or from can	30 mL
2 tbsp	lemon juice	30 mL
1 tbsp	tamari or soy sauce	15 mL
1	clove garlic, chopped	1
1/2 tsp	ground cumin	2 mL
Pinch	cayenne pepper	Pinch
2 tbsp	chopped fresh parsley	30 mL

Combine beans, liquid, lemon juice, tamari, garlic, cumin and cayenne in bowl of food processor and purée until smooth. Add parsley and blend for 5 seconds.

Makes 1-1/2 cups (375 mL)

PER 1/2-CUP (125 mL) SERVING

calories 168
protein 11 g
fat 0.5 g
carbohydrate 32 g
dietary fiber 7 g
sodium 275 mg

Excellent source of:
iron, magnesium, folate
Good source of:
thiamin
Source of:
calcium, zinc, riboflavin, omega-3 fatty acids

% Calories from:
protein 25%
fat 3%
carbohydrate 72%

Raw Vegetable Platter

Serve a platter filled with colorful cut-up vegetables:

- to encourage your family to eat their veggies when they come in from school or work
- as an attractive way of serving any of these foods at mealtimes
- as a low-cal, healthy snack while watching TV
- as an artistic accompaniment to festive meals
- as a great way to get vitamins, antioxidants, phytochemicals and fiber.

Here's a list of veggies you can serve raw, on their own or with one of the dips or spreads in this chapter:

- asparagus tips
- broccoli florets
- carrot sticks
- cauliflower florets
- celery sticks
- cherry tomatoes
- cucumber slices
- green onions
- green beans
- jicama sticks
- mushrooms
- sliced or whole, parsnip sticks
- red, yellow and green pepper strips
- snow peas
- sweet potato strips (dipped into water with a little lemon juice to prevent browning)
- turnip strips
- yam strips
- zucchini strips.

CURRY SANDWICH SPREAD

This mild curry sandwich filling has the look and texture of egg salad. The recipe makes enough for 4 sandwiches and it can be served as an appetizer with raw vegetables, crackers or bread.

1 lb	medium-firm tofu, pressed	454 g
1/4 cup	mayonnaise, tofu (recipe page 87) or low-fat	60 mL
1 tbsp	chopped green onion	15 mL
1 tbsp	chopped fresh parsley	15 mL
2 tsp	tamari or soy sauce	10 mL
1/2 tsp	curry powder	2 mL
1/2 tsp	chili powder	2 mL
1/2 tsp	nutritional yeast	2 mL
1/4 tsp	garlic powder	1 mL
	Salt and pepper	

PER 1/2-CUP (125 mL) SERVING

calories 96
protein 10 g
fat 5 g
carbohydrate 3 g
dietary fiber 0.3 g
sodium 181 mg

Good source of:
omega-3 fatty acids
Source of:
calcium, iron, thiamin

% Calories from:
protein 40%
fat 46%
carbohydrate 14%

Press tofu, as described on page 44, for 20 minutes. Discard liquid. Mash tofu in bowl with fork. Stir in mayonnaise, onion, parsley, tamari, curry powder, chili powder, yeast, garlic powder, and salt and pepper to taste.

Makes 2 cups (500 mL)

Gee Whiz Spread

Here's a tasty, easy-to-make spread, without the saturated fat and cholesterol of cheese, from *The Uncheese Cookbook*, by Joanne Stepaniak (published by The Book Publishing Company). It's great with veggie burgers to make "cheezeburgers," on crackers and in sandwiches.

1-1/2 cups	Great Northern beans (cooked or canned)	375 mL
1/2 cup	chopped pimiento or roasted bell pepper, page 53	125 mL
6 tbsp	nutritional yeast	90 mL
3 tbsp	fresh lemon juice	45 mL
2-3 tbsp	tahini	30-45 mL
1/2 tsp	onion powder	2 mL
1/2 tsp	prepared yellow mustard	2 mL
1/2 tsp	salt	2 mL

In bowl of food processor, blend beans, pimiento, yeast, lemon juice, tahini, onion, mustard and salt until smooth. Chill thoroughly before serving.

Makes 2 cups (500 mL)

Scrambled Tofu,
recipe page 43

ROASTED RED BELL PEPPERS

Roasting bell peppers accentuates the sweetness of the naturally occurring sugars of the vegetable. The charring that occurs when they are roasted adds a slight smoky flavor. Roasted peppers can replace pimientos in the recipes for Gee Whiz, page 52. and Cashew Lasagna, page 105–6. Roasted peppers can also be cut into strips and served on a platter with a drizzle of extra virgin olive or flaxseed oil, fresh herbs and a splash of lemon juice or vinegar. Cut them into julienne strips and use as a topping for the Veggie Pepperoni Pizza, page 134. Cut into squares they could be introduced to the Pasta and Vegetable Salad, page 72, or the Cumin and Currant Pilaf, page 109.

Choose peppers that are flat and have even surfaces rather than those that are curved and gnarly. Wash and set the peppers on the top rack directly under broiler heat. Turn them occasionally with a pair of tongs until they begin to char and appear cooked, about 5 to 8 minutes. Transfer the peppers to a bowl and insert into a plastic bag so the peppers steam. This will make peeling the peppers easier once they are cool enough to handle. With a paring knife, remove the skin from the peppers, cut off the top, slice the pepper in half and remove the seeds. Cut peppers into strips and use according to the chosen recipe. Peppers will keep for two days in the refrigerator.

VARIATION:
Try yellow or orange bell peppers in place of red peppers.

Crispy Fried Tofu, recipe page 125,
with Tofu Mayonnaise, recipe page 87

Gooda Cheeze

Gooda Cheeze is the clever creation of Joanne Stepaniak, author of *The Uncheese Cookbook* and *Table for Two*. The agar dissolves after simmering for a few minutes, then cools to form a firm gel, so that Gooda Cheeze can be sliced into wedges. Please see page 173 for information regarding agar.

PER 1/4-CUP (60 mL) SERVING

calories 68
protein 2 g
fat 2 g
carbohydrate 2 g
dietary fiber 0.4 g
sodium 126 mg

Excellent source of:
riboflavin, thiamin
Source of:
magnesium, folate,
vitamin A

% Calories from:
protein 13%
fat 61%
carbohydrate 26%

Note that although the percentage of calories from fat appears high, the total calories and grams of fat per serving are actually both low, about one-third that of gouda cheese.

1-3/4 cups	water	425 mL
1/2 cup	chopped carrot	125 mL
1/3 cup	agar flakes	75 mL
1/2 cup	raw cashew pieces	125 mL
1/4 cup	nutritional yeast	60 mL
3 tbsp	tahini	45 mL
3 tbsp	fresh lemon juice	45 mL
1 tbsp	Dijon mustard	15 mL
2 tsp	onion powder	10 mL
1 tsp	salt	5 mL
1/2 tsp	garlic powder	2 mL
1/2 tsp	dry mustard	2 mL
1/4 tsp	each turmeric, paprika and ground cumin	1 mL

In covered saucepan, bring water, carrots and agar to boil, lower heat and simmer 10 minutes.

Pour carrot mixture into blender and add cashews, yeast, tahini, lemon juice, mustard, onion powder, salt, garlic powder, mustard, turmeric, paprika and cumin, processing until very smooth. Pour immediately into lightly oiled 3-cup (750 mL) bowl or mold with rounded bottom. Cover and chill several hours or overnight. To serve, turn out of mold and slice into wedges.

Makes 3 cups (750 mL)

Hummus

Hummus, or the lower fat Black Bean Hummus, can be a staple and perhaps even replace your jar of peanut butter. It is a thoroughly nourishing spread to keep near the front of the refrigerator for hungry children and teens.

2 cups	cooked chick-peas	500 mL
1/3 cup	tahini	75 mL
1/3 cup	lemon juice	75 mL
1/3 cup	cooking water from chick-peas	75 mL
2	cloves garlic, chopped	2
1 1/2 tsp	ground cumin	7 mL
1/2 tsp	salt (less if using canned beans)	2 mL
1/8 tsp	toasted sesame oil	0.5 mL
Pinch	cayenne	Pinch
3 tbsp	chopped fresh parsley	45 mL
1-2 tbsp	extra-virgin olive oil (optional)	15-30 mL

In bowl of food processor, combine chick-peas, tahini, lemon juice, cooking water, garlic, cumin, salt, sesame oil and cayenne. Purée until smooth, occasionally scraping down sides of bowl. Add parsley and olive oil (if using), and blend for 30 seconds. Adjust seasoning.

Makes 2-1/2 cups (625 mL)

PER 1/2-CUP (125 mL) SERVING

calories 227
protein 9 g
fat 12 g
carbohydrate 23 g
dietary fiber 5 g
sodium 292 mg

With 2 tbsp olive oil:
calories 262
fat 16 g

Excellent source of:
iron, magnesium, zinc, folate
Source of:
calcium, thiamin

% Calories from:
protein 16%
fat 45%
carbohydrate 39%

With 2 tbsp olive oil:
% Calories from:
protein 13%
fat 54%
carbohydrate 33%

MOROCC-UN-BUTTER

Here's a spicy North African spread, with more nutritional value than butter or margarine, and without cholesterol or trans-fatty acids. The base is tahini, a sesame seed butter. Some brands of tahini are drier than others: if you find that your butter is too stiff, add up to 1 tbsp (15 mL) of vegetable stock or water to thin it out.

PER TABLESPOON
(15 mL)

calories 49
protein 2 g
fat 4 g
carbohydrate 2 g
dietary fiber 1 g
sodium 18 mg

Source of:
iron, magnesium,
thiamin

% Calories from:
protein 11%
fat 74%
carbohydrate 15%

1/2 cup	tahini	125 mL
3-4 tbsp	lemon juice	45-60 mL
3 tbsp	chopped green onions	45 mL
2 tbsp	chopped fresh parsley	30 mL
2 tbsp	chopped fresh cilantro	30 mL
1-2	cloves garlic	1-2
1 1/2 tsp	ground cumin	7 mL
1 tsp	paprika	5 mL
1 tsp	tamari or soy sauce	5 mL
1/4 tsp	chili powder or paste (optional)	1 mL

In bowl of food processor, combine tahini, lemon juice, onions, parsley, cilantro, garlic, cumin, paprika, tamari and chili (if using). Blend until smooth.

Makes 1 cup (250 mL)

ROASTED GARLIC AND YAM SPREAD

This fat-free spread is packed with the protective antioxidant beta-carotene, also known as vitamin A. Its deep orange color makes it very attractive served with crackers, vegetable sticks or assorted breads such as pumpernickel, rye, wheat or sourdough.

3	small yams (unpeeled)	3
2	cloves garlic (unpeeled)	2
1 1/2 tsp	lemon juice	7 mL
1 tsp	nutritional yeast	5 mL
1/4 tsp	oregano	1 mL
1/4 tsp	salt	1 mL
Pinch	pepper	Pinch
1 tbsp	chopped fresh parsley	15 mL

PER 1/3 RECIPE

calories 126
protein 2 g
fat 0.2 g
carbohydrate 30 g
dietary fiber 4 g
sodium 191 mg

Excellent source of:
riboflavin, thiamin,
vitamins A and C
Good source of:
folate
Source of:
iron, magnesium

% Calories from:
protein 8%
fat 1%
carbohydrate 91%

Roast yams and garlic in 275°F (135°C) oven until soft, about 45 minutes. Set aside until cool enough to handle. Squeeze out garlic with thumb and index finger and peel yams, then transfer to bowl of food processor. Add lemon juice, yeast, oregano, salt and pepper; purée until smooth. Add parsley and purée for 5 seconds.

Makes about 1-1/3 cups (325 mL)

Sun-Dried Tomato Pesto

A little bowl of pesto, served with crackers or fresh bread, adds such a wonderful flavor and aroma of basil to a festive occasion.

Per 2 tbsp
(30 mL) serving

calories 46
protein 1 g
fat 4 g
carbohydrate 3 g
dietary fiber 1 g
sodium 105 mg

Good source of:
thiamin
Source of:
magnesium

% Calories from:
protein 10%
fat 68%
carbohydrate 22%

1/2 cup	sun-dried tomatoes	125 mL
2/3 cup	fresh basil leaves	150 mL
1/2 cup	pine nuts	125 mL
1	clove garlic, chopped	1
1 tbsp	lemon juice	15 mL
1 tsp	nutritional yeast	5 mL
1/4 tsp	salt	1 mL
Pinch	pepper	Pinch

Soak tomatoes overnight in 1 cup (250 mL) cold water (or pour boiling water over them to get the same result in 4 hours). In bowl of food processor, purée tomatoes, basil, pine nuts, garlic, lemon juice, yeast, salt and pepper until smooth. If mixture is too thick, add 1 to 2 tbsp (15 to 30 mL) of vegetable stock, tomato juice or water.

Makes 3/4 cup (175 mL)

GOMASIO

Sprinkled over vegetables, soups or cooked grains and beans,
Gomasio deepens the overall flavor of a dish. It is a perfect
alternative to using salt at the table. Look for dulse or kelp powders
at your local health food store.

Note: To grind this amount of seeds all at once, you need a
mortar that has a 2-inch (5 cm) deep bowl and a 3-1/2-inch (9 cm)
wide mouth. If your mortar is smaller, crush seeds in batches.
Alternatively, use a small electric grinder.

PER 1/2 TSP
(2 mL) SERVING

calories 9
protein 0.3 g
fat 1 g
carbohydrate 0.3 g
dietary fiber 0.1 g
sodium 22 mg

% Calories from:
protein 12%
fat 73%
carbohydrate 15%

1/2 cup	hulled sesame seeds	125 mL
1/2 tsp	salt	2 mL
1/4 tsp	dulse powder or kelp powder	1 mL

Dry-roast sesame seeds in skillet over medium heat for 5 to 7 minutes, stirring frequently, until seeds can be crushed between your
thumb and finger. Transfer to mortar or food grinder. Add salt and
dulse. Using pestle and grinding in circular motion or using pulse
action of the grinder, grind seeds until most of them are crushed
(approximately 75 percent), and coated with their own oil. Store in
sealed jar in refrigerator for several weeks.

Makes 1/2 cup (125 mL)

TOASTED SUNFLOWER SEEDS

These seeds make a savory alternative to deep fried potato or corn chips. Easy to make, they are a good snack for hungry children and adults at home, on the trail or at the lake. They can also be used as a garnish for salads, baked potatoes and cooked grains.

2 cups	sunflower seeds	500 mL
2 tbsp	nutritional yeast	30 mL
2 tsp	tamari or soy sauce	10 mL

Spread seeds evenly on baking sheet and bake in 350°F (180°C) oven for 10 to 12 minutes.

Transfer seeds to large bowl, stir in yeast and tamari and toss to coat evenly.

Let cool before transferring to jar with lid. Seeds keep for 1 week on the shelf, or 2 to 3 weeks refrigerated (if they are around that long!).

Makes 2 cups (500 mL)

WHAT WILL I SPREAD ON MY BREAD OR TOAST?

Which is the lesser of two evils, butter or margarine? If you've become tired of this debate, opt for something that can offer some nutritional pluses found in neither. For example, almond butter is a tasty source of calcium. Cashew butter provides you with zinc. Gee Whiz Spread is high in nutritional value, yet low in calories. And all the recipes listed below offer wonderfully satisfying flavor.

- Almond butter, cashew butter or other nut and seed butters
- Black Bean Hummus (page 49)
- Curry Sandwich Spread (page 51)
- Debrah's Avocado Dip (page 48)
- Fruit jam
- Gee Whiz Spread (page 52)
- Gooda Cheeze (page 54)
- Hummus (page 55)
- Miso, thinly spread
- Morocc–un–Butter (page 56)
- Roasted Garlic and Yam Spread (page 57)
- Sesame tahini, with blackstrap molasses or honey (a thin layer of each)
- Sun-Dried Tomato Pesto (page 58)

SALADS

APPLE WALNUT SALAD

This is a pretty salad for festive occasions, or even to cheer you up on a rainy day! The salad is a mound of lettuce, sprouts, pepper and apple slices, surrounded by a circle of orange slices and walnuts. Serve it with Orange Mint (page 84) or with a raspberry dressing. The salad provides your day's supply of omega-3 fatty acids.

PER SERVING

calories 125
protein 4 g
fat 8 g
carbohydrate 13 g
dietary fiber 3 g
sodium 8 mg

Excellent source of:
folate, vitamins C and
E, omega-3 fatty acids
Good source of:
magnesium, vitamin A
Source of:
calcium, iron, zinc,
riboflavin, thiamin

% Calories from:
protein 10%
fat 53%
carbohydrate 37%

1/3	sweet red bell pepper	1/3
1/3	sweet green bell pepper	1/3
1/2	small red apple	1/2
1 tbsp	lemon juice	15 mL
5 cups	leafy green lettuce, torn into bite-sized pieces	1.25 L
1 cup	alfalfa sprouts	250 mL
1	orange, peeled and thinly sliced crosswise	1
1/2 cup	walnut halves	125 mL

Cut top and bottom from peppers, remove seeds and cut peppers lengthwise into 1/4-inch (5 mm) strips. Slice apple into quarters, core and cut lengthwise into 1/4-inch (5 mm) slices. Toss in lemon juice to keep from turning brown. Toss lettuce, peppers and sprouts together in large bowl. Form a mound of tossed salad on large platter. Arrange orange slices and walnuts at base of salad. Garnish salad with apple slices.

Makes 4 servings

BASMATI RICE SALAD

Basmati is an aromatic rice, grown in the foothills of the Himalayas. Sweet raisins, mild curry and the nutty taste of basmati rice colorfully combine to make a truly delicious salad. For the quick-cooking version described here, you may use white basmati rice, or use the longer-cooking brown basmati as described in the variation.

1/2 cup	raisins, soaked in 1/2 cup (125 mL) water	125 mL
3-3/4 cups	water	925 mL
2 cups	white basmati rice	500 mL
3 tbsp	soaking water from raisins	45 mL
2-3 tbsp	mild curry paste	30-45 mL
2 tbsp	lemon juice	30 mL
1 tsp	salt	5 mL
1/2 cup	finely diced red pepper	125 mL
1/2 cup	chopped parsley	125 mL
1 tsp	coriander seed, crushed	5 mL

PER CUP (250 mL)

calories 291
protein 6 g
fat 3 g
carbohydrate 62 g
dietary fiber 2 g
sodium 365 mg

Excellent source of:
magnesium, folate
Good source of:
iron, vitamins A
and C
Source of:
calcium, zinc, thiamin

% Calories from:
protein 7%
fat 10%
carbohydrate 83%

Soak raisins in enough water to cover for 30 minutes.

Bring 3-3/4 cups (925 mL) water to boil, pour in rice, cover, reduce heat to simmer and cook for 20 minutes. Transfer rice to medium bowl and allow to cool.

Combine raisin water, curry paste, lemon juice and salt and mix well. Stir curry mixture into rice, along with red pepper, parsley and coriander seed.

Drain liquid from raisins and add raisins to rice. Gently mix with fork.

VARIATION:
Use brown basmati in place of white and cook for 45 minutes.

Makes 6 cups (1.5 L)

CALCIUM-RICH GREENS

Kale can be eaten both raw, as in this recipe, or steamed. When eaten raw, it is best sliced very fine, due to its fibrous nature. In this salad, which provides 135 mg calcium per 50-calorie portion, kale is combined with Chinese cabbage (also known as *sui choy* or napa cabbage) and broccoli, two other greens chosen for their high calcium availability. Oriental Dressing (page 85) or Lemon Tahini Dressing (page 83) complements this salad.

PER SERVING

calories 50
protein 4 g
fat 1 g
carbohydrate 10 g
dietary fiber 4 g
sodium 59 mg

Excellent source of:
folate, vitamins A
and C
Good source of:
magnesium
Source of:
calcium, iron,
riboflavin, thiamin,
omega-3 fatty acids

% Calories from:
protein 24%
fat 9%
carbohydrate 67%

2 cups	kale	500 mL
2 cups	Chinese cabbage	500 mL
2-1/2 cups	broccoli florets and peeled, sliced stem	625 mL
1 cup	diced sweet red pepper	250 mL

Remove kale from stem and slice leaves matchstick thin. Cut cabbage leaves in half lengthwise and slice into 1/2-inch (1 cm) strips. Combine kale, Chinese cabbage, broccoli and diced red pepper.

Makes 4 servings

Caesar Salad

Here's a healthier version of a perennial favorite. Drying the lettuce leaves as much as possible after washing serves two functions. It lets the dressing cling to the leaves, and it removes water that would otherwise dilute a very flavorful dressing.

DRESSING:

1	pkg (10 oz/300 g) soft silken tofu	1
2-3	cloves garlic	2-3
1/3 cup	lemon juice	75 mL
2 tbsp	capers	30 mL
4 tsp	Dijon mustard	20 mL
1/2 tsp	salt	2 mL
1/8 tsp or less	freshly cracked black pepper	0.5 mL
2 tbsp	extra virgin olive oil (optional)	30 mL

Drain water from tofu package and empty tofu into a food processor or blender. Add garlic, lemon juice, capers, mustard, salt and pepper and purée until smooth. If using oil, pour in very slowly. Adjust seasoning.

Makes 1-3/4 cups (425 mL) dressing.

SALAD:

1	head romaine lettuce	1
1-1/2 cups	croutons	375 mL
1/2 cup	Caesar dressing	125 mL
2-4 tbsp	grated soy or dairy Parmesan cheese	30-60 mL

Lay head of romaine on cutting board. Cut romaine to make bite-size pieces 1 inch (2.5 cm) square. Rinse lettuce in cold water and spin or pat dry with clean tea towel. Place leaves in large bowl and toss with croutons and dressing until leaves are coated. Sprinkle with cheese.

Makes 4 servings

PER SERVING

calories 122
protein 7 g
fat 5 g
carbohydrate 15 g
dietary fiber 2 g
sodium 555 mg

With oil in dressing:
calories 148
fat 7 g

Excellent source of:
folate, vitamins A and C
Good source of:
iron, thiamin
Source of:
calcium, magnesium, zinc, niacin, riboflavin, vitamin E, omega-3 fatty acids

% Calories from:
protein 22%
fat 32%
carbohydrate 46%

With oil in dressing:
% Calories from:
protein 18%
fat 43%
carbohydrate 39%

COUSCOUS SALAD

Couscous, sometimes known as Moroccan pasta, is made from durum wheat that has had the bran and germ removed, been coarsely ground and precooked. Dishes using this refined wheat product are very quick to prepare. Here it is colorfully combined with currants, sweet red pepper and parsley.

PER SERVING

calories 153
protein 5 g
fat 2 g
carbohydrate 29 g
dietary fiber 3 g
sodium 275 mg

Source of:
iron, magnesium, zinc,
folate, niacin, thiamin,
vitamin E

% Calories from:
protein 12%
fat 14%
carbohydrate 74%

1/4 cup currants, soaked in 1/4 cup (60 mL) hot water		60 mL
1 cup	couscous	250 mL
1 cup	water	250 mL
1/2 tsp	salt	2 mL
1 tbsp	tahini	15 mL
1 tbsp	lemon juice	15 mL
1/4 cup	diced sweet red pepper	60 mL
2 tbsp	chopped fresh parsley	30 mL
1/2 tsp	coriander seeds, crushed	2 mL
1/2 tsp	ground cumin	2 mL
Pinch	pepper	Pinch

Soak currants in hot water for 10 to 15 minutes. Meanwhile, measure couscous into bowl.

Bring water and salt to boil, then pour over couscous. Cover bowl with plate to keep in heat and set aside to cool completely.

Mix tahini and lemon juice together in small bowl; stir into couscous. Drain currants and add to couscous along with diced red pepper, parsley, coriander, cumin and pepper. Gently toss with fork.

Makes 4 servings

DEEP GREEN LEAFY SALAD

The contrasting colors in this salad – light green lettuce, dark green kale and bright red pepper strips – make a lovely presentation, tossed in a bowl or served on a platter, accompanied by any of the dressings in this book. You'll see in the analysis that salad vegetables provide about 10% calories from plant oils, including healthful omega-3 fatty acids.

4 cups	torn leafy lettuce	1 L
3-4 cups	thinly sliced kale	750 mL-1 L
1/2	each sweet red and yellow peppers	1/2
1 cup	grated carrots	250 mL
1/2 cup	grated red radish (optional)	125 mL
2 cups	alfalfa sprouts	500 mL

Wash lettuce, spin-dry and tear into bite-size pieces. Place in large bowl. Remove kale leaves from stem and slice leaves matchstick thin. Discard stems and add leaves to bowl. Seed red and yellow peppers. Cut into 1/4-inch (5 mm) strips.

Set aside for garnish 1/3 of each of red and yellow peppers, grated carrots and radish (if using); add remainder to bowl and toss.

Garnish top of salad with reserved peppers, carrots and radishes. Arrange alfalfa sprouts around edge.

Makes 6 servings

PER SERVING

calories 45
protein 3 g
fat 1 g
carbohydrate 9 g
dietary fiber 3 g
sodium 27 mg

Excellent source of:
vitamins A, C and E
Good source of:
folate
Source of:
iron, magnesium,
calcium, zinc,
riboflavin, thiamin,
omega-3 fatty acids

% Calories from:
protein 20%
fat 10%
carbohydrate 70%

FRESH VEGETABLE SALAD ROLL

After the ingredients for this salad roll are laid out before you, the rolls can be assembled with ease. Different sauces such as Barbecue, Peanut (page 164), Lemon Tahini (page 83), Teriyaki (page 166) or Plum, inside the roll as well as for dipping create a deliciously wide range of flavor possibilities. Try experimenting with different ingredients for the filling such as replacing avocado with Crispy Fried Tofu (page 125).

1	rice paper sheet, 8-1/2-inch (21 cm) round	1
8 cups	warm water in large bowl	2 L
1/3 cup	cooked brown rice	75 mL
1 tsp	Barbecue Sauce	5 mL
2 tbsp	grated carrot	30 mL
3	slices avocado	3
1	6-inch (15 cm) strip green onion, sliced lengthwise	1
1/2 tsp	minced fresh coriander	2 mL
1/2 tsp	julienned pickled gingerroot (optional)	2 mL

Dip one sheet of rice paper into water for 5 seconds then place on cutting board. Pat with dry cloth to absorb any excess water.

Spread rice on paper in a square leaving 1-inch (2.5 cm) border free on all sides. Layer sauce, carrot, avocado, green onion, coriander and ginger along bottom portion of rice.

Fold right and left margins toward the center followed by the bottom margin. Moisten top margin of paper. Using both hands, tightly roll the paper toward the top. Apply a bit of pressure with hands to seal roll.

Makes one roll

DAVID'S GARDEN OF PLENTY SALAD

Vesanto's husband, David, spends half an hour several times a week assembling this salad. Stored in a couple of large, well-sealed containers, it will last for 3 or 4 days. In this case, the romaine is best added fresh every 2 days. Alternatively, this recipe will also feed a big hungry family in one sitting. It is excellent with the Oriental Dressing (page 85) and the Lemon Tahini Dressing (page 83).

5	leaves kale	5
5	leaves romaine	5
5	leaves Chinese cabbage	5
1/4	head red cabbage	1/4
1	stalk broccoli	1
1/2	small head cauliflower	1/2
3-4	carrots	3-4
1	red pepper	1

Remove stem from kale and cut kale into matchsticks. Tear lettuce into bite-size pieces. Cut Chinese cabbage leaves in half lengthwise, and slice into 1/4-inch (5 mm) strips. Slice red cabbage into thin slices. Cut broccoli and cauliflower into bite-size florets. Stem of broccoli can be peeled and diced. Slice carrots and cut red pepper into 1/4-inch (5 mm) strips. Toss all in bowl.

Makes 10 servings

PER SERVING

calories 51
protein 3 g
fat 0.5 g
carbohydrate 10 g
dietary fiber 4 g
sodium 68 mg

Excellent source of:
folate, vitamins A, C and E
Source of:
calcium, iron, magnesium, riboflavin, thiamin, omega-3 fatty acids

% Calories from:
protein 23%
fat 8%
carbohydrate 69%

PASTA AND VEGETABLE SALAD

In this recipe the cooked vegetables are blanched until firm to the bite but not entirely cooked.

1 cup	diagonally sliced carrots	250 mL
1 cup	snow peas	250 mL
1 cup	broccoli or cauliflower florets	250 mL
2-1/2 cups	uncooked pasta, such as colored shells	625 mL
1	sweet red pepper, diced	1
1 cup	sliced mushrooms	250 mL
1	chopped green onion	1

DRESSING:

1/4 cup	rice vinegar	60 mL
2 tbsp	sesame oil	30 mL
1 tbsp	tamari	15 mL
2 tsp	grated ginger	10 mL
1/4 tsp	toasted sesame oil (optional)	1 mL
1	clove garlic, minced	1

PER SERVING

calories 178
protein 5 g
carbohydrate 30 g
fat 4 g
dietary fiber 3 g
sodium 118 mg

Excellent source of:
thiamin, vitamins A and C, omega-3 fatty acids
Good source of:
iron, folate, riboflavin
Source of:
magnesium, zinc, niacin, vitamin E

% Calories from:
protein 12%
fat 22%
carbohydrate 67%

In large pot of boiling water, cook carrots 5 minutes. Add snow peas and broccoli, cook for 2 more minutes until tender crisp. Remove from pot with slotted spoon or strainer and plunge into cold water to arrest cooking. Return water to boil and cook pasta for 8 to 10 minutes or until al dente. Drain vegetables and pasta very well.

In blender, combine vinegar, oil, tamari, ginger, and garlic.

In bowl, toss cooked vegetables, pasta, pepper, mushrooms, onions and dressing together. Refrigerate 1 hour to blend flavors before serving.

Makes 4 servings

PICKLED BEET AND KALE SALAD

The contrast of red and green in this salad is pleasing to the eye. The acid in vinegar keeps red vegetables bright. Balsamic vinegar is an excellent choice; however, raspberry, red wine or apple cider vinegars or lemon juice are delightful as well. The pickled beets are also good served without the kale, and will keep in the refrigerator for up to 4 days.

4	beets	4
1/4 cup	balsamic vinegar	60 mL
1/4 tsp	caraway seeds	1 mL
1/4 tsp	salt	1 mL
Pinch	ground cloves	Pinch
4 cups	chopped kale	1 L
1 tbsp	chopped fresh parsley (optional)	15 mL
Pinch	freshly ground pepper	Pinch

Cover beets with cold water in pot. Bring to boil, reduce to simmer and cook 20 to 40 minutes (depending on size) or until a skewer easily slips out of beet when pierced. Allow beets to cool in cooking liquid. Peel beets under cold running water by squeezing skins so they slip off.

Slice beets; place in bowl and add vinegar, caraway seeds, salt and cloves. Set aside for at least 1 hour in refrigerator, tossing to mix occasionally.

Remove stems from kale. Discard stems and slice leaves very thin. Steam over medium-high heat for 3 minutes. Spread warm greens on serving platter and arrange beets over top. Garnish with parsley (if using) and pepper.

Makes 4 servings

PER SERVING

calories 65
protein 3 g
fat 1 g
carbohydrate 13 g
dietary fiber 4 g
sodium 202 mg

Excellent source of:
folate, vitamins A
and C
Good source of:
magnesium
Source of:
calcium, iron,
riboflavin, thiamin,
omega-3 fatty acids

% Calories from:
protein 19%
fat 8%
carbohydrate 73%

POTATO DILL SALAD

Compare the nutritional analysis when this salad is made with the Tofu Mayonnaise on page 87 and with the regular commercial type.

4	unpeeled potatoes	4
1/3 cup	mayonnaise (tofu or low-fat commercial)	75 mL
2 tbsp	diced celery	30 mL
2 tbsp	chopped green onions	30 mL
2 tbsp	chopped fresh parsley	30 mL
1 tsp	Dijon mustard	5 mL
1/2 tsp	dillweed	2 mL
1/4 tsp	paprika	1 mL
1/4 tsp	salt	1 mL
Pinch	pepper	Pinch

In pot of boiling water, cook potatoes over medium heat for 20 minutes or until tender. Drain and cool under cold running water. Stir together mayonnaise, celery, onions, parsley, mustard, dill, paprika, salt and pepper in bowl. Cube potatoes; stir into mayonnaise mixture and gently toss with fork.

Makes 4 servings

VARIATION:

Add one or two diced Polski Ogorki or garlic dill pickles.

QUINOA SALAD WITH LIME DRESSING

Quinoa (pronounced keen-wa) is an ancient grain native to the high Andes regions of South America, and recently introduced to the Canadian prairies. It is often called a "supergrain" because of its excellent protein. When harvested it is coated with a resin that is generally removed before it is marketed. Some quinoa that you buy will need to be rinsed in a strainer until the foamy resin is washed away.

3 cups	cooked quinoa or	750 mL
1-1/2 cups	water and	375 mL
1 cup	raw quinoa	250 mL
1/2 cup	peeled, seeded and diced cucumber	125 mL
1/2 cup	cooked corn kernels (fresh, canned or frozen)	125 mL
1/4 cup	diced sweet red pepper	60 mL
2 tbsp	finely chopped green onion	30 mL
4 tsp	finely chopped cilantro	20 mL

If using raw quinoa, bring water to a boil, add quinoa, cover, lower heat and simmer for 15 to 20 minutes or until water is absorbed. Let cool. In bowl, combine quinoa, cucumber, corn, red pepper, green onion and cilantro.

LIME DRESSING:

3 tbsp	lime juice	45 mL
3 tbsp	canola oil (optional)	45 mL
1/2 tsp	toasted sesame oil	2 mL
1/2 tsp	salt	2 mL
Pinch	pepper	Pinch

In small bowl combine lime juice, canola oil (if using), sesame oil, salt and pepper. Pour over quinoa mixture and toss gently. Adjust seasoning. Refrigerate for 1 to 3 hours before serving to let flavors blend.

Makes 3 servings

PER SERVING

calories 188
protein 6 g
fat 3 g
carbohydrate 36 g
dietary fiber 3 g
sodium 278 mg

With canola oil:
calories 278
fat 13 g

Excellent source of:
iron, magnesium (and omega-3 fatty acids with canola oil)
Source of:
zinc, folate, niacin, riboflavin, thiamin, vitamin A

% Calories from:
protein 13%
fat 14%
carbohydrate 73%

With canola oil:
% Calories from:
protein 10%
fat 36%
carbohydrate 54%

SUN-DRIED TOMATO & RICE SALAD

When tomatoes are dried they develop a wonderful sweetness and tang. Keep a little bag of them in your kitchen cupboard and they will often come in handy to add flavor and color to grains, salads, pastas and many other dishes.

PER SERVING

calories 319
carbohydrate 51g
fat 11 g
protein 6 g
sodium 300 mg

Excellent source of:
magnesium
Good source of:
niacin, thiamin,
vitamin E
Source of:
iron, zinc, folate,
vitamin C

% Calories from:
protein 8%
fat 29%
carbohydrate 63%

1/4 cup	dry sun-dried tomatoes	60 mL
4 cups	cooked brown rice, cooled	1 L
1/4 cup	tomato sauce	60 mL
2 tbsp	sunflower seeds	30 mL
2 tbsp	chopped parsley	30 mL
2 tbsp	extra-virgin olive oil	30 mL
2 tbsp	lemon juice	30 mL
2 tsp	chopped fresh basil	30 mL
1/4 tsp	garlic powder	1 mL
1/4 tsp	salt	1 mL
Pinch	black pepper	Pinch

Soak tomatoes in 1/2 cup (250 mL) cold water for a minimum of 4 hours, drain well and chop. In medium bowl combine rice, sun-dried tomatoes, tomato sauce, sunflower seeds and parsley.

In small bowl mix olive oil, lemon juice, basil, garlic powder, salt and pepper. Pour over rice and gently toss with fork. Adjust seasoning to taste.

Makes 4 servings

WATERCRESS, AVOCADO AND GRAPEFRUIT SALAD

The dressing for this elegant salad uses mirin – a Japanese rice wine which is subtle, delicious and clean to the palate. The grapefruit juice can be squeezed from the remaining pulp after the segments are removed from the fruit.

1/3	bunch watercress	1/3
2	ripe avocados	2
1	grapefruit	1
1/2 tsp	Gomasio (page 59)	2 mL

DRESSING:

2 tbsp	grapefruit juice	30 mL
2 tbsp	mirin	30 mL
2 tsp	rice vinegar	10 mL
1/2 tsp	tamari	2 mL

PER SERVING

calories 190
protein 3 g
fat 15 g
carbohydrate 13 g
dietary fiber 5 g
sodium: 50 mg

Excellent source of:
folate, vitamins C and
E, omega-3 fatty acids
Good source of:
magnesium
Source of:
iron, niacin, riboflavin,
thiamin, vitamin A

% Calories from:
protein 5%
fat 67%
carbohydrate 27%

Wash and dry watercress; arrange 3 to 4 stems on top third of 4 plates. Set aside. Cut avocado in half lengthwise and remove pit. Carefully remove pulp in one piece using a soup spoon.

To fan avocado make thin strips lengthwise starting 1/2 inch down from narrow end through to the bottom. With pressure from hand and at a 45° angle, push avocado so that it fans out. Arrange avocado fan on bed of greens so that the fanned area is near the bottom of the plate.

Slice top and bottom from grapefruit. Using sharp knife, slice skin and pith away to expose fruit. Cut along both sides of segments towards center to loosen them and remove. Garnish each plate with 2 segments to form an X on either side of the avocado.

DRESSING:
Squeeze juice from pulp into small bowl. Measure juice, mirin, vinegar and tamari. Spoon 1 tbsp of dressing on each salad.

Sprinkle salad with pinch of Gomasio.

Makes 4 servings

DRESSINGS

CUCUMBER DILL DRESSING

In the heat of summer, cucumbers are so blessedly cooling. Serve this dressing with tender leafy greens, vine-ripened tomatoes or use it as a dip with veggies or pita bread.

Per 2 tbsp (30 mL)

calories 12
protein 1 g
fat 1 g
carbohydrate 1 g
dietary fiber 0.1 g
sodium 9 mg

With oil:
calories 26
fat 2 g

% Calories from:
protein 29%
fat 39%
carbohydrate 32%

With oil:
% Calories from:
protein 14%
fat 71%
carbohydrate 15%

1	pkg (10 oz/300 g) soft silken tofu	1
1 cup	peeled, seeded, chopped cucumber	250 mL
1/4 cup	lemon juice	60 mL
1	small clove garlic	1
1 tsp	Dijon mustard	5 mL
3/4 tsp	dillweed	4 mL
2 tbsp	extra-virgin olive oil (optional)	30 mL
	Salt and pepper	

In food processor, combine drained tofu, cucumber, lemon juice, garlic, mustard and dillweed; purée until smooth. Add oil (if using), and seasoning and blend for 10 seconds. Store in refrigerator in covered container for up to 2 weeks.

Makes 2 cups (500 mL)

FLAXSEED OIL-TOMATO-BASIL DRESSING

A tablespoon of this dressing will meet the Canadian recommendations for omega-3 fatty acids for three days. This recipe was developed using Omega Nutrition's top quality flaxseed oil. The classic combination of garlic, basil and tomatoes makes it a favorite to serve with Green Leafy Salad (page 69), or over steamed vegetables. It keeps well in the refrigerator.

1/4 cup	apple cider vinegar	60 mL
3–5	cloves garlic	3–5
3 tbsp	fresh basil (or 1 tbsp dried)	45 mL
1–2 tbsp	sun-dried tomatoes	15–30 mL
1 tsp	Dijon mustard	5 mL
1 tsp	tamari or soy sauce (optional)	5 mL
1/2 tsp	each oregano and tarragon	2 mL
1/2 tsp	maple syrup	2 mL
6	drops Tabasco	6
3/4 cup	flaxseed oil	175 mL

Soak tomatoes in 1/4 cup (60 mL) hot water for 1 hour. Drain. In food processor or blender, combine vinegar, garlic, basil, sundried tomatoes, mustard, tamari (if using), oregano, tarragon, maple syrup and Tabasco; blend until smooth. Slowly add oil in steady continuous stream.

Makes 1 cup (250 mL)

GREENS SALAD DRESSING

Here's a good reason to grow green herbs on your balcony, kitchen windowsill or in the garden. This light salad dressing allows you to savor the full burst of flavor of these herbs. It only keeps a day or two and is best made fresh.

Per 2 tbsp (30 mL)

calories 22
protein 0.4 g
fat 2 g
carbohydrate 1 g
dietary fiber 0.2 g
sodium 104 mg

Excellent source of:
omega-3 fatty acids

% Calories from:
protein 7%
fat 71%
carbohydrate 22%

3/4 cup	water	175 mL
2 tsp	rice flour	10 mL
1 cup	chopped fresh parsley	250 mL
1/2 cup	chopped fresh cilantro	125 mL
2 tbsp	chopped fresh basil	30 mL
1 tbsp	lemon juice	15 mL
1 tbsp	tamari or soy sauce	15 mL
1 tbsp	flaxseed oil	15 mL
1	small clove garlic, chopped	1
1/2	green onion, chopped (optional)	1/2

Stir water and rice flour together in pot over high heat and bring to boil. Reduce heat and simmer for 3 minutes. Remove from heat and transfer to blender. Add parsley, coriander, basil, lemon juice, tamari, flaxseed oil, garlic and green onion (if using); blend for 1 to 2 minutes. Pour into jar and let cool before covering with lid.

Makes 1-1/4 cup (300 mL)

VARIATION:

For a creamier dressing, add 1/4 cup of mayonnaise (tofu, page 87 or commercial).

Lemon Tahini Dressing

A delicious sesame seed butter, tahini can be used to flavor sauces and soups, or to give creamy texture in a dressing like this one. Flavors vary from brand to brand so look for one that appeals to you. Since tahini is not hydrogenated, oil may rise to its surface during storage; stir before using.

1/3 cup	plain soy milk or water	75 mL
2 tbsp	lemon juice	30 mL
1 tsp	tamari or soy sauce	5 mL
1	small clove garlic, chopped	1
1/4 tsp	salt	1 mL
Pinch	pepper	Pinch
1/4 cup	tahini	60 mL

Blend soy milk, lemon juice, tamari, garlic, salt and pepper in blender or food processor. Add tahini and blend for 15 seconds or until smooth.

Makes 3/4 cup (175 mL)

Per 2 tbsp (30 mL)

calories 68
protein 2 g
fat 6 g
carbohydrate 3 g
dietary fiber 1 g
sodium 136 mg

Good source of:
magnesium
Source of:
iron, zinc, folate, thiamin

% Calories from:
protein 12%
fat 73%
carbohydrate 15%

ORANGE MINT DRESSING

What a concept – a salad dressing without any oil! The mixture of mint and orange complements Apple Walnut Salad (page 64) and any salad of leafy greens and sprouts. Rice syrup is a very mild sweetener found in health food stores or Oriental markets.

PER 2 TBSP (30 ML)

calories 43
protein 1 g
fat 0.1 g
carbohydrate 10 g
dietary fiber 0.2 g
sodium 50 mg

Excellent source of:
vitamin C
Good source of:
folate
Source of:
thiamin

% Calories from:
protein 6%
fat 1%
carbohydrate 93%

1 cup	frozen orange juice concentrate	250 mL
1/2 cup	water	125 mL
1 tbsp	apple cider vinegar	15 mL
1 tsp	rice syrup or honey	5 mL
1 tsp	dried mint	5 mL
1/2 tsp	dried coriander	2 mL
1/4 tsp	salt	1 mL
1/8 tsp	pepper	0.5 mL

Combine orange juice concentrate, water, vinegar, rice syrup, mint, coriander, salt and pepper in jar and shake until blended. Keep in refrigerator for 2 weeks.

Makes 1-1/3 cups (325 mL)

Curried Vegetables with Tofu,
recipe page 110
Spinach with Garam Masala,
recipe page 156

ORIENTAL DRESSING

Rice vinegar is a delicate vinegar with about half the acidity of
other vinegars. The combination of rice vinegar and rice syrup with
toasted sesame oil and the five spices in the Chinese seasoning –
cinnamon, fennel, anise, star anise and pepper – makes an intriguing
blend in this favorite recipe developed by Vesanto. Serve with
Calcium-Rich Greens on page 66 or as a marinade for tofu.

PER 2 TBSP (30 mL)

calories 74
protein 0.1 g
fat 3 g
carbohydrate 13 g
dietary fiber 0 g
sodium 21 mg

% Calories from:
protein 0%
fat 34%
carbohydrate 66%

1/4 cup	rice vinegar	60 mL
1/4 cup	rice syrup	60 mL
1 tbsp	water	15 mL
1 tbsp	sesame or canola oil	15 mL
1	clove garlic, minced	1
1 tsp	grated peeled gingerroot	5 mL
1/4 tsp	toasted sesame oil	1 mL
1/8 tsp	Chinese 5-spice seasoning	0.5 mL

In jar with lid, shake rice vinegar, rice syrup, water, oil, garlic, ginger,
toasted sesame oil and 5-spice seasoning for 15 seconds or until rice
syrup is dissolved.

Makes 2/3 cup (150 mL)

Deep Green Leafy Salad,
recipe page 69, with
Flaxseed Oil–Tomato-Basil Dressing,
recipe page 81

TOFU MARINADE

Tofu takes on other flavors very easily, hence its exceptional versatility. Here's a marinade to use with tofu or tempeh for stir fries or barbecues; pour 1/2 cup (125 mL) over block of firm tofu or tempeh that has been cut into bite-size cubes. It's also delicious as a light salad dressing or simply served over brown rice.

Per 2 tbsp (30 mL)

calories 25
protein 1 g
fat 2 g
carbohydrate 1 g
dietary fiber 0.1 g
sodium 477 mg

% Calories from:
protein 15%
fat 67%
carbohydrate 18%

1/2 cup	canned tomatoes	125 mL
1/2 cup	tamari or soy sauce	125 mL
1/2 cup	water	125 mL
1/4 cup	apple cider vinegar	60 mL
2 tbsp	toasted sesame oil	30 mL
1 tsp	chopped garlic	5 mL
1 tsp	grated, peeled gingerroot	5 mL
1/2 tsp	turmeric	2 mL

In blender, purée tomatoes, tamari, water, vinegar, sesame oil, garlic, ginger and turmeric; blend for 10 seconds until smooth.

Transfer to jar with tight-fitting lid. This marinade keeps in refrigerator for 2 to 3 weeks.

Makes 1-3/4 cups (425 mL)

TOFU MAYONNAISE

Here's an excellent eggless mayo you can easily make using firm silken tofu. Experiment by adding a few capers, green onions, cilantro, garlic or soaked sun-dried tomatoes to make your favorite yummy mayo.

I	pkg (10 oz/300 mL) firm silken tofu	I
2 tbsp	lemon juice	30 mL
2 tbsp	brown rice syrup or 1 tbsp honey	30 mL
2 tsp	rice vinegar	10 mL
2 tsp	extra-virgin olive oil (optional)	10 mL
1 tsp	prepared mustard	5 mL
3/4 tsp	nutritional yeast	4 mL
1/4 tsp	salt	I mL

Drain tofu; place in food processor and blend for 1 minute, occasionally scraping down sides of bowl. Add lemon juice, rice syrup, vinegar, olive oil (if using), mustard, yeast and salt; blend for 30 seconds until smooth. Store in refrigerator in covered container for up to 2 weeks.

Makes 1-1/4 cups (300 mL)

PER 2 TBSP (30 ML)

calories 37
protein 3 g
fat 1 g
carbohydrate 5 g
dietary fiber 0 g
sodium 122 mg

With olive oil:
calories 45
fat 2 g

Source of:
riboflavin, thiamin

% Calories from:
protein 30%
fat 20%
carbohydrate 50%

With olive oil:
% Calories from:
protein 25%
fat 35%
carbohydrate 40%

TOMATO-HERB DRESSING

This recipe can be varied according to your preferred herbs to create healthy, low-oil dressings. The tomato juice provides body and considerably reduces the amount of oil required. Try different herbs such as oregano or dill, on their own or in combination. If you use dried herbs instead of fresh, use one third the amount specified for fresh herbs. You may also substitute apple cider vinegar for lemon juice, or tomato-vegetable juice for tomato juice.

PER 2 TBSP (30 ML)

calories 29
protein 0.1 g
fat 3 g
carbohydrate 1 g

Excellent source of:
omega-3 fatty acids
when made with
flaxseed oil

% Calories from:
protein 3%
fat 80%
carbohydrate 17%

1 cup	tomato juice	250 mL
2 tbsp	lemon juice	30 mL
2 tbsp	apple cider vinegar	30 mL
2 tbsp	extra-virgin olive oil, flaxseed oil or mixture of both	30 mL
1-1/2 tsp	chopped fresh basil	7 mL
1 tsp	Dijon mustard	5 mL
1/2 tsp	dried tarragon (optional)	2 mL
pinch	pepper	pinch

In jar with lid, combine tomato juice, lemon juice, oil, basil, mustard, tarragon (if using) and pepper; shake for 30 seconds. Store in refrigerator for up to a week.

Makes 1-1/4 cups (300 mL)

SOUPS

BLACK BEAN SOUP

Black beans are a tasty Mexican staple and can be used in salads, stews and soup. The cumin and oregano give a southern accent to this soup. Adding lime juice just before serving adds a bright note.

4 cups	vegetable stock	1 L
1 tbsp	canola oil (optional)	15 mL
1 cup	diced carrot	250 mL
1 cup	diced celery	250 mL
1/2	onion, diced	1/2
1	clove garlic, minced	1
3 cups	cooked black turtle beans or black beans	750 mL
1/4 cup	tomato paste	60 mL
1-1/2 tsp	ground cumin	7 mL
1 tsp	dried oregano	5 mL
1 tsp	dried thyme	5 mL
2 tsp	lime juice	10 mL
	Salt and pepper	

Sauté carrot, celery, onion and garlic in 2 tbsp (30 mL) of the stock, adding more stock if necessary, or 1 tbsp (15 mL) oil in large pot over medium heat for 5 minutes. Stir in beans, remaining stock, tomato paste, cumin, oregano and thyme. Cover and simmer for 20 minutes or until vegetables are cooked. Just before serving, stir in lime juice. Stir in salt and pepper to taste.

Makes 4 servings

CARROT AND YAM SOUP

Certain vitamins and phytochemicals in vegetables provide the splendid array of colors you see when you walk down the produce aisle. Three of these vitamins are bright yellow: riboflavin, folate and vitamin A, also known as beta-carotene. This warming, golden soup is packed with all three!

4 cups	vegetable stock	1 L
1 tbsp	canola oil (optional)	15 mL
4 cups	chopped carrots	1 L
2 cups	peeled and chopped yam	500 mL
1/2	small onion, sliced	1/2
1-1/2 tsp	peeled, sliced gingerroot	7 mL
1 cup	apple juice	250 mL
2 tbsp	orange juice concentrate	30 mL
1 tsp	dried coriander	5 mL
1/4 tsp	allspice	1 mL
1/4 tsp	nutmeg	1 mL
1/4-1/2 tsp	salt	1-2 mL
Pinch	pepper	Pinch

PER SERVING

calories 224
protein 4 g
fat 1 g
carbohydrate 52 g
dietary fiber 7 g
sodium 259 mg

With oil:
calories 254
fat 4 g

Excellent source of:
vitamins A, C and E
Good source of:
iron, magnesium,
folate, riboflavin
Source of:
calcium, zinc, niacin,
thiamin

% Calories from:
protein 7%
fat 3%
carbohydrate 90%

With oil:
% Calories from:
protein 6%
fat 14%
carbohydrate 80%

Sauté carrots, yams, onion and ginger in 2 tbsp (30 mL) of the stock, adding more stock if necessary, or 1 tbsp (15 mL) oil in large pot over medium heat for 3 to 5 minutes.

Stir in remaining stock, apple juice, orange juice concentrate, coriander, allspice, nutmeg, salt and pepper; reduce heat and simmer until carrots are soft. Transfer to food processor or blender and purée until smooth. Return to pot to reheat and adjust seasoning.

Makes 4 servings

CREAMY VEGETABLE SOUP

Tahini makes this hearty soup extra creamy. Broccoli, kale and Chinese cabbage have become favorites of many people because the calcium in these greens is highly available to the body. This soup provides iron, zinc and magnesium as well.

6 cups	water	1.5 L
1/2 cup	brown rice	125 mL
1	clove garlic, minced	1
1 tsp	peeled grated gingerroot	5 mL
1 cup	each diced carrots and zucchini	250 mL
1 cup	each sliced broccoli, Chinese cabbage and kale	250 mL
1/3 cup	tahini	75 mL
2 tbsp	tamari or soy sauce	30 mL
2 tbsp	miso (optional)	30 mL
Pinch	cayenne (optional)	Pinch
1 tbsp	diced green onion	15 mL

In covered pot, combine water, rice, garlic and ginger; simmer for 45 minutes. Add carrots; cook for 5 minutes. Add zucchini, broccoli, cabbage and kale; cook for 5 more minutes.

In small bowl, combine tahini, tamari, miso and cayenne (if using) along with 1/2 cup (125 mL) of liquid from soup; mix into smooth paste. Add to soup.

Adjust seasoning and garnish with green onions.

Makes 4 servings

LENTIL SOUP

Adapted from *The Moosewood Cookbook*, by Mollie Katzen (Ten Speed Press), this recipe takes considerably less time than the original; however, the taste is still spectacular. Thank you, Mollie!

4 cups	vegetable stock	1 L
1 tbsp	canola oil (optional)	15 mL
1/2	onion, chopped	1/2
1	large clove garlic, minced	1
2 cups	fresh or canned tomatoes, chopped	500 mL
1 cup	dried lentils	250 mL
1 tsp	dried oregano	5 mL
1 tsp	dried basil	5 mL
2	bay leaves	2
1 cup	diced carrots	250 mL
1 cup	diced celery	250 mL
2 tbsp	blackstrap molasses or brown sugar	30 mL
1 tbsp	apple cider vinegar	15 mL
1/4–1/2 tsp	salt	1–2 mL
1/8 tsp	pepper	0.5 mL

PER SERVING

calories 239
protein 15 g
fat 1 g
carbohydrate 46 g
dietary fiber 9 g
sodium 220 mg

With oil:
calories 268
fat 4 g

Excellent source of:
iron, magnesium,
folate, thiamin,
vitamins A and C
Good source of:
calcium, zinc,
vitamin E
Source of:
niacin, riboflavin

% Calories from:
protein 24%
fat 3%
carbohydrate 72%

With oil:
% Calories from:
protein 22%
fat 14%
carbohydrate 64%

Sauté onion and garlic in 2 tbsp (30 mL) stock, adding more stock if necessary, or 1 tbsp (15 mL) oil in large pot over medium heat for 5 minutes.

Stir in remaining stock, tomatoes, lentils, oregano, basil and bay leaves. Cover and simmer for 45 minutes. Add carrots, celery, molasses, vinegar, salt and pepper; cook for 12 to 15 minutes or until vegetables are tender–crisp. Remove bay leaves. Adjust seasoning.

Makes 4 servings

MINESTRONE SOUP

When he was banquet chef at the Vancouver Four Seasons Hotel, Joseph made this soup in 100 L batches. This version serves only four and has a no-oil option, but it can be made with the same attention to detail as in any fine dining establishment.

Per serving

calories 162
protein 6 g
fat 2 g
carbohydrate 35 g
dietary fiber 7 g
sodium 286 mg

With oil:
calories 191
fat: 5 g

Excellent source of:
magnesium, folate,
vitamins A and C
Good source of:
iron, thiamin,
vitamin E
Source of:
calcium, zinc, niacin,
riboflavin,

% Calories from:
protein 14%
fat 8%
carbohydrate 78%

With oil:
% Calories from:
protein 12%
fat 21%
carbohydrate 67%

4 cups	vegetable stock	1 L
1 tbsp	olive oil (optional)	15 mL
1 cup	each diced carrots, celery and potato	250 mL
1/2	large onion, diced	1/2
2	cloves garlic, minced	2
2 cups	chopped fresh or canned tomatoes	500 mL
2 tbsp	tomato paste	30 mL
1 tsp	dried basil	5 mL
1/2 tsp	dried oregano	2 mL
1/4 tsp	celery seeds	1 mL
1/4-1/2 tsp	salt	1-2 mL
Pinch	pepper	Pinch
1 cup	each sliced zucchini and green or yellow beans	250 mL
1/2 cup	cooked garbanzo, kidney or white beans	125 mL
2 tbsp	chopped parsley	30 mL

Sauté carrots, celery, onions and garlic in 2 tbsp (30 mL) of the stock, adding more stock if necessary, or 1 tbsp (15 mL) oil in large pot over medium heat for 5 minutes. Stir in potato, remaining stock, tomatoes, tomato paste, basil, oregano, celery seeds, salt and pepper. Cover, reduce heat and simmer for about 10 minutes or until potatoes are half-cooked. Add zucchini, green beans, and your choice of legumes. Cover and cook for about 5 to 7 minutes or until vegetables are tender-crisp. Adjust seasoning and garnish with parsley.

Makes 4 servings

MISO SOUP

Miso is a rich, thick, fermented soybean paste from Japan, where it is credited with many healthful qualities. Depending on the grain used in combination with soybeans and the length of fermentation, each miso has its own distinct aroma, flavor, color and use. Lighter miso is sweeter and better for summer use while darker miso is more robust and suited to the colder months.

PER SERVING

calories 65
protein 4 g
fat 2 g
carbohydrate 8 g
dietary fiber 1 g
sodium 850 mg *(one third of maximum recommended day's intake)*

Source of:
iron, magnesium, zinc, folate, omega-3 fatty acids

% Calories from:
protein 24%
fat 28%
carbohydrate 48%

4-1/2 cups	water	1.125 L
1/4 cup	thinly sliced gingerroot (unpeeled)	60 mL
1	small clove garlic, chopped	1
1/3 cup	miso	75 mL
2 tbsp	mirin	30 mL
2 tbsp	chopped green onion	30 mL
2 tbsp	finely diced firm tofu	30 mL

Simmer water, ginger and garlic in large pot over medium heat for 10 minutes. Strain liquid, discarding ginger and garlic, then return liquid to pot. Combine miso, mirin and 1 cup (250 mL) of stock in small bowl, mixing with fork until miso is dissolved. Stir miso mixture into pot; add tofu and green onion. Heat but do not boil.

VARIATION:

For a more substantial soup, after liquid is strained, add 1/2 cup (125 mL) sliced carrot, 1/2 cup (125 mL) thinly sliced Chinese cabbage, 1/4 cup (60 mL) sliced snow peas and 2 tbsp (30 mL) sliced green onion and simmer for 5 to 7 minutes or until tender-crisp. Add miso as described above.

Makes 4 servings

Mulligatawny Soup

In one of the languages of Southern India, mulligatawny means "pepper water." The spiciness varies according to how much pepper and ginger you add, so if you like it hot, add more, as this version is mild. The sweetness of apple and celery balances the spice.

4 cups	vegetable stock	1 L
1 tbsp	canola oil (optional)	15 mL
1 cup	sliced celery	250 mL
1	apple, diced	1
1/2	onion, diced	1/2
1 tsp	peeled, minced gingerroot	5 mL
1	clove garlic, minced	1
1 tbsp	tomato paste	15 mL
1-1/2 tsp	curry powder	7 mL
1/4 tsp	celery seeds	1 mL
1/4 tsp	salt	1 mL
1/8-1/4 tsp	black pepper	0.5-1 mL
1/4 cup	white basmati rice	60 mL

Sauté celery, apple, onion, ginger and garlic in 2 tbsp (30 mL) of the stock, adding more stock if necessary, or 1 tbsp (15 mL) oil in large pot over medium heat for 5 minutes.

Stir in tomato paste, curry powder, celery seeds, salt and pepper. Cook for 5 minutes, stirring frequently to prevent sticking. Add remaining stock and basmati rice. Bring to a boil, cover, reduce heat and simmer for 30 minutes, stirring occasionally. Adjust seasoning.

Makes 4 servings

MUSHROOM BROTH

Mushrooms blend well with marjoram and thyme. With the variety of mushrooms on the market today – regular field, crimini, oyster, shiitake and Portobello – this soup can have a number of variations. Vegetable stock is essential in this recipe; dissolve vegetable bouillon cubes or powder in warm water or make your own from scratch.

6 cups	vegetable stock	1.5 L
1 tbsp	canola oil (optional)	15 mL
4 cups	thinly sliced fresh mushrooms	1 L
4	green onions, chopped	4
1/2 tsp	dried marjoram	2 mL
1/4 tsp	dried thyme	1 mL
1/4 tsp	salt	1 mL
1/8 tsp	pepper	0.5 mL
1 tbsp	chopped parsley	15 mL

Sauté mushrooms in 2 tbsp (30 mL) of the stock, adding more stock if necessary, or 1 tbsp (15 mL) oil in large pot over medium heat for 5 minutes or until they start to brown. Add remaining stock, green onions, marjoram, thyme, salt and pepper; simmer for 10 minutes. Adjust seasoning. Divide broth among 4 serving bowls. Garnish with parsley.

Makes 4 servings

SPICY EGGPLANT SOUP

This soup makes a warming and aromatic meal, accompanied by a slice of bread with Morocc-un-Butter, page 56. The spiciness can be heightened by increasing the ginger or pepper.

7 cups	vegetable stock	1.75 L
1 tbsp	olive oil (optional)	15 mL
2	carrots, diced	2
2	potatoes, diced	2
1	onion, diced	1
1	eggplant, cubed	1
2 tbsp	grated peeled gingerroot	30 mL
2	cloves garlic, minced	2
1 cup	chopped fresh or canned tomatoes	250 mL
1/2 cup	chopped fresh cilantro	125 mL
1 tsp	cumin	5 mL
1/2 tsp	pepper	2 mL
	Salt	

In large soup pot, sauté carrots, potatoes, onion, eggplant, ginger and garlic over medium heat in 2 tbsp (30 mL) stock, adding more if necessary, or 1 tbsp (15 mL) oil for 3 to 5 minutes or until onions are soft.

Stir in remaining stock, tomatoes, cilantro, cumin and pepper; cover, bring to boil, then lower heat and simmer for 20 to 30 minutes or until potatoes are cooked. Adjust seasoning.

Makes 6 servings

SPLIT PEA SOUP WITH VEGGIE BACK BACON

Yves Potvin of Yves Veggie Cuisine has developed a number of completely plant-based meat analogs that are exceptional in quality. His Veggie Back Bacon has a delicate smoked flavor that adds a wonderful base note to this recipe. Served with a wholesome bread and salad, this soup easily satisfies the heartiest appetites.

8 cups	vegetable stock	2 L
1 tbsp	canola oil (optional)	15 mL
1 cup	diced carrot	250 mL
1 cup	diced celery	250 mL
1/2	onion, diced	1/2
2	cloves garlic, minced	2
2 cups	dried green split peas, rinsed	500 mL
3	bay leaves	3
5	whole cloves	5
1/4-1/2 tsp	salt	1-2 mL
1/8 tsp	black pepper	0.5 mL
3	slices Yves Veggie Back Bacon	3
1 tbsp	chopped fresh parsley	15 mL

Sauté carrots, celery, onion and garlic in 2 tbsp (30 mL) of the stock, adding more stock if necessary, or 1 tbsp (15 mL) oil in large pot over medium heat for 5 minutes. Stir in remaining stock, split peas, bay leaves and cloves. Bring to boil, cover, reduce heat and simmer for 45 to 60 minutes. Add salt, pepper, Veggie Back Bacon and more water if soup is too thick.

Remove bay leaves before serving. Garnish with parsley; adjust seasoning.

Makes 6 servings

PER SERVING

calories 260
protein 17 g
fat 1 g
carbohydrate 45 g
dietary fiber 7 g
sodium 241 mg

With oil:
calories 279
fat 3 g

Excellent source of:
iron, magnesium, folate, thiamin, vitamin A
Good source of:
zinc
Source of:
calcium, niacin, riboflavin

% Calories from:
protein 26%
fat 3%
carbohydrate 71%

With Oil:
% Calories from:
protein 24%
fat 10%
carbohydrate 66%

VEGETABLE NOODLE SOUP

Freshly crushed coriander seeds give this soup a unique twist. Its pleasant aromatic taste suggests a mixture of caraway and cumin. Combined here with carrots and yams, a sweetness comes through that is subtle and nourishing.

1/2 cup	spiral, shell or elbow noodles	250 mL
4 cups	vegetable stock	1 L
1 tbsp	canola oil (optional)	15 mL
1/2 cup	each diced carrot, celery, turnip and yam	125 mL
1/2	onion, diced	1/2
1	clove garlic, minced	1
2 tbsp	chopped fresh parsley	30 mL
1 tsp	crushed coriander seeds	5 mL
1/4-1/2 tsp	salt	1-2 mL
Pinch	pepper	Pinch

Cook noodles according to package directions and set aside.

Sauté carrot, celery, turnip, yam, onion and garlic in 2 tbsp (30 mL) of the stock, adding more stock if necessary, or 1 tbsp (15 mL) canola oil in large pot over medium heat for 5 minutes. Add remaining stock, parsley and coriander seeds; cover and simmer for 15 minutes or until vegetables are tender-crisp. Add noodles, salt and pepper; adjust seasoning.

Makes 4 servings

VEGETABLE STOCK

This simple stock can be kept on hand in the refrigerator for 4–5 days or made in larger quantities and frozen. Try substituting different vegetables such as tomatoes, fennel, leeks and mushrooms or herbs such as basil, rosemary and coriander. Avoid cabbage family vegetables in your stock as their taste and odor are overpowering.

6 cups	water	1.5 L
2	carrots, diced	2
2	stalks celery, diced	2
1	large onion, chopped	1
1/4 cup	parsley leaves and stems	60 mL
2	large cloves garlic, chopped	2
1/2 tsp	dried thyme	1 mL
10	peppercorns, crushed	10
3	bay leaves	3
3	whole cloves	3

Place water, carrots, celery, onion, parsley, garlic, thyme, peppercorns, bay leaves and cloves in large pot; bring to simmer and cook, uncovered, for 30 minutes. Strain through colander or sieve, discard vegetables and let stock cool before refrigerating or freezing.

Makes 6 cups (1.5 L)

ENTRÉES

AFRICAN STEW

Peanut butter makes a wonderful, creamy sauce for this nutrition-packed stew. Lemon juice, added at the end, gives a lively nuance to the flavor. Season with a dash of hot pepper sauce, fiery chipotle sauce or Vietnamese chili sauce.

PER SERVING

calories 385
protein 13 g
fat 11 g
carbohydrate 63 g
dietary fiber 8 g
sodium 354 mg

Excellent source of:
magnesium, folate,
vitamins A and E
Good source of:
iron, zinc, niacin,
riboflavin, thiamin
Source of:
calcium

% Calories from:
protein 13%
fat 24%
carbohydrate 63%

4 cups	vegetable stock	1 L
1	onion, chopped	1
2	cloves garlic, minced	2
2 cups	peeled diced yams	500 mL
1 cup	cooked chick-peas	250 mL
1/2 cup	brown rice	125 mL
1/4 tsp	salt	1 mL
1/4 cup	peanut butter	60 mL
2 cups	chopped kale	500 mL
2 tbsp	lemon juice	30 mL
	tamari or soy sauce (optional)	
	chili sauce	

In large pot over medium heat, sauté onion and garlic in 2 tbsp (30 mL) of vegetable stock for 3 to 5 minutes or until onions are soft. Add remaining stock, yams, chick-peas, rice and salt; simmer, covered, for 45 minutes.

In small bowl, blend peanut butter and 1/2 cup (125 mL) of liquid from stew to make smooth paste. Stir into stew along with kale, cook for 5 minutes. Stir in lemon juice, tamari (if using) and chili sauce to taste. Adjust seasoning.

Makes 4 servings

Cashew Cheese Lasagna

Cashews provide a wonderful cheesy-tasting topping for this lasagna.
Pimiento can be added to the cashew cheese to give an orange
color. A lot of salt is added during the processing of canned tomato
products, so if you're trying to lower your sodium intake, try one of
the low-sodium tomato sauces available.

6	lasagna noodles	6
2	pkg (each 10 oz/300 g) extra-firm silken tofu	2
2 tbsp	vegetable stock or water	30 mL
2 cups	chopped mushrooms	500 mL
1 cup	diced celery	250 mL
1	onion, diced	1
1 tsp	each dried basil and oregano	5 mL
1/2 tsp	salt	2 mL
1/8 tsp	pepper	0.5 mL
1-1/2 cups	tomato sauce	375 mL
1	large tomato, sliced	1

Cashew Cheese:

1-1/2 cups	raw, unsalted cashew pieces	375 mL
1-1/2 cups	water	375 mL
1/3 cup	nutritional yeast	75 mL
1/3 cup	lemon juice	75 mL
4 tsp	tamari or soy sauce	20 mL
2 tsp	onion powder	10 mL
1 tsp	celery seed	5 mL
1/2 tsp	garlic powder	2 mL
1/2 cup	sweet pimientos (optional)	125 mL

Per serving

calories 320
protein 17 g
fat 17 g
carbohydrate 32 g
dietary fiber 4 g
sodium 576 mg

Excellent source of:
iron, magnesium, zinc,
folate, riboflavin,
thiamin, vitamin E
Good source of:
omega-3 fatty acids
Source of:
calcium, niacin,
vitamin A

% Calories from:
protein 19%
fat 44%
carbohydrate 37%

Cashew Cheese:

Blend cashews, water, yeast, lemon juice, tamari, onion powder,
celery seed, garlic powder and pimientos (if using) in blender for
1 minute or until very smooth.

LASAGNA:

Cook noodles according to package directions. Drain and cool in cold running water. Meanwhile, mash tofu in large bowl.

In skillet over medium heat, sauté mushrooms, celery and onion in stock for 5 minutes or until onions are soft, adding more stock or water if necessary. Transfer to bowl with tofu along with basil, oregano, salt and pepper, stirring to mix.

TO ASSEMBLE:

Spread 1/3 cup (75 mL) of tomato sauce in lightly oiled 13- x 9-inch (3 L) baking dish. Lay 3 noodles over sauce. Spoon half of tofu mix over noodles followed by remaining tomato sauce, remaining noodles and tofu mixture. Pour Cashew Cheese as final layer and spread evenly over filling. Top with tomato slices and bake at 350°F (180°C) for 30 to 40 minutes or until Cashew Cheese has set and moisture bubbles along the sides of pan.

Makes 8 servings

EAST INDIAN CHICK-PEAS

Once you've discovered Indian curry pastes, you'll enjoy the ease with which you can put together a vegetable or bean curry. Even the mild pastes are hot enough for most people. The Patak brand is our favorite. Use a little or a lot, depending on your preference.

1	onion, diced	1
2	cloves garlic, minced	2
2 cups	chopped fresh or canned tomatoes	500 mL
1 tbsp	canola oil (optional)	15 mL
1–3 tsp	mild curry paste	5–15 mL
3 cups	cooked chick-peas	750 mL
1 tbsp	lemon juice	15 mL
1 tsp	tamari or soy sauce	5 mL
1/4 tsp	salt (optional)	1 mL

Sauté onion and garlic in 2 tbsp (30 mL) of liquid from tomatoes, adding more liquid if necessary, or 1 tbsp (15 mL) oil in skillet over medium heat for 3 to 5 minutes or until onions are soft. Stir in curry paste and cook for 3 minutes, adding more juice from tomatoes if it becomes too dry. Add tomatoes, chick-peas, lemon juice and tamari; cook for 15 minutes. Season to taste.

Makes 4 servings

PER SERVING

calories 254
protein 13 g
fat 4 g
carbohydrate 44 g
dietary fiber 8 g
sodium 90 mg

With oil:
calories 276
fat 8 g

Excellent source of:
iron, magnesium,
folate, vitamin C
Good source of:
zinc, thiamin,
vitamin E
Source of:
calcium, niacin,
riboflavin, vitamin A,
omega-3 fatty acids

% Calories from:
protein 19%
fat 15%
carbohydrate 66%

With oil:
% Calories from:
protein 17%
fat 23%
carbohydrate 60%

CHILI WITH TEXTURED SOY PROTEIN

When iron-rich foods such as kidney beans or textured soy protein are eaten with vitamin C-rich foods such as tomatoes, onions and peppers, the body's absorption of iron is greatly increased.

PER SERVING

calories 240
protein 16 g
fat 2 g
carbohydrate 45 g
dietary fiber 14 g
sodium 219 mg

Excellent source of:
iron, magnesium,
folate, thiamin,
vitamins A and C
Good source of:
zinc, riboflavin,
vitamin E
Source of:
calcium, niacin,
omega-3 fatty acids

% Calories from:
protein 25%
fat 6%
carbohydrate 69%

2 cups	vegetable stock	500 mL
1 cup	each diced carrots, celery and green peppers	250 mL
1/2	onion, diced	1/2
2	cloves garlic, minced	2
1 tbsp	canola oil (optional)	15 mL
2 cups	cooked or canned kidney beans, drained	500 mL
2 cups	chopped fresh or canned tomatoes	500 mL
1/4 cup	tomato paste	60 mL
1/2 cup	textured soy protein	125 mL
1 tsp	each ground cumin, dried basil, chili powder	5 mL
1/4 tsp	black pepper	1 mL
2	bay leaves	2
	Salt and pepper	
2 tbsp	chopped fresh cilantro	30 mL

In large covered pot, sauté carrots, celery, green peppers, onion and garlic in 2 tbsp (30 mL) water over medium heat for 5 minutes or until onions are soft.

Stir in beans, tomatoes, stock, tomato paste, textured soy protein, cumin, basil, chili powder, pepper and bay leaves; bring to boil then reduce heat, cover and simmer 20 minutes.

Adjust seasoning. Remove bay leaves. Garnish with cilantro.

VARIATION:

Textured soy protein may be replaced by uncooked medium-grade bulgur.

Makes 4 servings

CURRANT AND CUMIN PILAF

Small sweet grapes, dried to form currants, are often an ingredient in Middle Eastern pilafs. Cumin combines here with currants and cloves to create a satisfying dish to serve with the Vegetable Kabobs on page 135.

4 cups	water	1 L
2 cups	brown rice	500 mL
2/3 cup	currants	150 mL
1 tsp	ground cumin	5 mL
1/2 tsp	salt	2 mL
1/4 tsp	turmeric	1 mL
6	whole cloves	6
1/4 cup	finely chopped green onion	60 mL

Boil water in covered pot over high heat; add rice, currants, cumin, salt, turmeric and cloves. Cover, reduce heat and cook for 45 minutes. Just before serving, stir in green onions.

Makes 4 hearty servings

PER SERVING

calories 415
protein 9 g
fat 3 g
carbohydrate 90 g
dietary fiber 5 g
sodium 284 g

Excellent source of:
magnesium, thiamin
Good source of:
iron, zinc, niacin
Source of:
folate, riboflavin

% Calories from:
protein 8%
fat 6%
carbohydrate 86%

CURRIED VEGETABLES WITH TOFU

Here is a rich dish with a coconut milk-based sauce to enjoy from time to time. It is designed to be served with basmati rice. For a change, make this curry without tofu and serve it with East Indian Chick-Peas (page 107). The crispy crackers called Papadums (see next page) are a great addition any time.

Per serving

calories 309
protein 14 g
fat 20 g
carbohydrate 25 g
dietary fiber 5 g
sodium 327 mg

Excellent source of:
iron, magnesium, folate, vitamins A and C
Good source of:
calcium, zinc, thiamin
Source of:
niacin, riboflavin

% *Calories from:*
protein 17%
fat 54%
carbohydrate 29%

1/4 cup	raisins	60 mL
1	onion, diced	1
1	clove garlic, minced	1
1 tsp	peeled, grated gingerroot	5 mL
1 tbsp	oil	15 mL
1 tsp	each curry powder and cumin	5 mL
1/2 tsp	each coriander, turmeric and salt	2 mL
1 cup	each diced carrots, red pepper	250 mL
1 cup	each chopped broccoli and cauliflower	250 mL
1 cup	firm tofu, diced	250 mL
7 oz	canned coconut milk	200 mL
2 tsp	lime juice	10 mL
1 tbsp	chopped fresh cilantro	15 mL
1/4 cup	unsalted cashews (optional)	60 mL

Cover raisins with water and let soak for 30 minutes. Sauté onion, garlic and ginger in oil over medium heat for 5 minutes. Stir in curry powder, cumin, coriander, turmeric and salt; sauté for 5 minutes.

Strain raisins and add to pan along with carrots, red pepper, broccoli, cauliflower, tofu and coconut milk; simmer until vegetables are tender and crisp. Stir in lime-juice, cilantro and cashews (if using).

Makes 6 servings

Papadums

Papadums are crispy, paper-thin crackers made with chick-pea flour and spices and are available at East Indian grocery stores. They can be mild or spicy depending on the type and amount of seasonings used. They can be eaten as an appetizer with chutney or as an accompaniment to a curry dinner. Normally deep fried when served in a restaurant, they have no added fat when prepared under a broiler.

To prepare them the no-fat way, preheat broiler and place oven rack 6 inches (15 cm) below broiler. Place 2 papadums on rack and broil, watching carefully. Once heat begins to blister papadum, move it around using tongs, until heat blisters every part of cracker (about 20 to 30 seconds). Turn papadum over.

Remove from oven once papadum is completely blistered on both sides.

CURRY IN A HURRY

Good-quality curry paste brings the rich spices of the East directly into your kitchen, allowing you to produce a tasty curry in minutes. Red lentils are the fastest-cooking legume and by serving them with white basmati rice, you can make a nourishing meal in less than 30 minutes. You may want to add leftover vegetables such as carrots, cauliflower or zucchini in the last 5 minutes of cooking.

PER SERVING

calories 186
protein 14 g
fat 2 g
carbohydrate 29 g
dietary fiber 7 g
sodium 10 mg

Excellent source of:
iron, folate
Good source of:
magnesium, zinc,
thiamin
Source of:
niacin, riboflavin

% Calories from:
protein 29%
fat 11%
carbohydrate 60%

2 tbsp	water	30 mL
1 cup	chopped tomato	250 mL
1/2	onion, diced	1/2
1	clove garlic, minced	1
1 tbsp	mild curry paste	15 mL
2-1/2 cups	water	625 mL
1 cup	dried red lentils	250 mL
1/4 tsp	salt	1 mL

Sauté tomato, onion, garlic and curry paste in 2 tbsp (30 mL) of water, adding more water if necessary, in pot over medium heat for 3 to 5 minutes. Stir in 2-1/2 cups (625 mL) water, lentils and salt; cover and simmer for 20 minutes. Adjust seasoning.

Makes 4 servings

FIGS AND BEANS
FABA IN FRIXORIO (BEANS IN THE FRYING PAN)

Who would have thought of combining figs, kidney beans and herbs? In fact, this dish was prepared by the famed 16th-century vegetarian Leonardo da Vinci (perhaps known to his friends as Leonardo da Veggie). In his delightful book *Famous Vegetarians and Their Favorite Recipes*, Rynn Berry describes this dish, as well as favorites from the days of Pythagoras, Plato and Socrates and up to modern times. The original instructions read: "In a greased frying pan combine cooked beans with onions, chopped figs, sage, garlic and various kitchen-garden herbs. Fry well in oil. Sprinkle with aromatic herbs and serve."

1 cup	dried figs	250 mL*
1 tbsp	olive oil	15 mL
1	onion, chopped	1
1	clove garlic, minced	1
3 cups	cooked kidney beans, drained	750 mL
1/4 tsp	each basil, thyme and rosemary	1 mL
Pinch	dried sage	Pinch
	Salt and pepper	
2 tbsp	chopped fresh parsley	30 mL

Soak figs in water for 12 hours. Reserve soaking liquid. Remove stems from figs, chop and set aside. Sauté onion and garlic in oil over medium heat for 5 minutes or until onions are soft. Add beans, figs, 1/2 cup (125 mL) soaking liquid, basil, thyme, rosemary and sage; cook on low heat for 10 minutes or until beans are heated through. Season to taste and stir in parsley.

Makes 4 servings

*Note that standardized teaspoons and metric measures were not used in 16th-century kitchens.

PER SERVING

calories 280
protein 13 g
fat 4 g
carbohydrate 51 g
dietary fiber 14 g
sodium 8 mg

Excellent source of:
iron, magnesium, folate
Good source of:
thiamin
Source of:
calcium, zinc, niacin, riboflavin, vitamin E

% Calories from:
protein 17%
fat 14%
carbohydrate 69%

INTERNATIONAL ROLL-UP

The basic roll-up begins with a 9-inch (23 cm) tortilla. It is a fabulous way of introducing exotic flavors into your menus – packed with nutrition, easy to make, and providing an opportunity to use leftovers. After trying a few variations, you'll discover your own favorite flavor combinations and before you know it, you'll be global-traveling on your lunch break. Gather and prepare all ingredients and lay them out on the counter. To assemble, spread a strip of rice on tortilla, followed by vegetables and sauce. Lift edge of tortilla and snugly roll.

FOR 1 INDONESIAN
ROLL-UP

calories 353
protein 17 g
fat 6 g
carbohydrate 67 g
dietary fiber 6 g
sodium 341 mg

Excellent source of:
iron, magnesium,
folate, vitamin C
Good source of:
zinc, niacin, thiamin,
vitamin A, omega-3
fatty acids
Source of:
calcium, riboflavin,
vitamin E

% Calories from:
protein 18%
fat 13%
carbohydrate 69%

INDONESIAN-STYLE

1/2 cup	cooked brown rice	125 mL
2 oz	Lemon Ginger Tempeh (page 117)	60 g
1/4 cup	sliced Chinese cabbage	60 mL
2 tbsp	sliced water chestnuts	30 mL
1 tsp	sliced pickled gingerroot	5 mL
2 tsp	Tamarind Date Sauce (page 165)	10 mL

AFRICAN-STYLE

1/3 cup	cooked brown rice	75 mL
1/3 cup	cooked mashed yam	75 mL
1/3 cup	sliced kale, lightly steamed	75 mL
2 tbsp	Peanut Sauce (page 164)	30 mL
1/4 cup	alfalfa sprouts	60 mL
Dash	hot pepper sauce	Dash

ITALIAN-STYLE

1/2 cup	cooked brown rice	125 mL
1/2 cup	raw spinach, steamed	125 mL
2	artichoke hearts, sliced	2
1 tsp	chopped fresh basil	5 mL
1	lettuce leaf	1
2 tbsp	tomato sauce	30 mL

JAPANESE-STYLE

1/2 cup	cooked brown rice	125 mL
1/4 cup	grated carrot	60 mL
1/4 cup	grated daikon radish	60 mL
2 tsp	mayonnaise (Tofu, page 87 or low-fat)	10 mL
2 tsp	sliced pickled gingerroot	10 mL
1/2 tsp	Gomasio (page 59)	2 mL
1	green onion, sliced thinly (green part)	1
2 tsp	Teriyaki Sauce (page 166)	10 mL

MEXICAN-STYLE

1/2 cup	cooked brown rice	125 mL
1/4 cup	grated carrot	60 mL
1/4 cup	shredded soy cheese or Cheddar	60 mL
1 tsp	chopped fresh cilantro	5 mL
2 tsp	mayonnaise (Tofu, page 87 or low-fat)	10 mL
1	lettuce leaf, cut into strips	1
2 tsp	salsa	10 mL

MIDDLE EASTERN-STYLE

1/2 cup	Hummus (page 55)	125 mL
1/4 cup	chopped fresh tomato	60 mL
1/4 cup	grated carrot	60 mL
1 tbsp	chopped fresh parsley	15 mL
1	lettuce leaf	1
2 tbsp	Lemon Tahini Dressing (page 183)	30 mL

LASAGNA AL FORNO

A new and improved version of an old standard, this savory lasagna, developed for Sunrise Soya Foods, has a filling that is made with tofu and topped with soy cheese. Serve it with the crunchy Caesar Salad (page 67) and a crusty loaf of bread for a satisfying meal for your family and guests.

PER SERVING

calories 222
protein 14 g
fat 8 g
carbohydrate 25 g
dietary fiber 3 g
sodium 352 mg

Excellent source of:
iron, magnesium,
folate, vitamin A
Good source of:
calcium, thiamin,
omega-3 fatty acids
Source of:
zinc, niacin, riboflavin,
vitamin E

% Calories from:
protein 24%
fat 32%
carbohydrate 44%

12 oz	extra-firm tofu, crumbled	350 g
2	bunches spinach, washed, cooked, drained and chopped	2
2/3 cup	soy cheese or dairy Parmesan cheese	150 mL
1 tsp	each onion powder, oregano and basil	5 mL
1/2 tsp	salt	1 mL
8 oz	soy cheese or low-fat mozzarella cheese (2-1/4 cups/550 mL grated)	240 g
1 tbsp	chopped fresh parsley	15 mL
1	can (28 oz/796 mL) tomato sauce	1
6	cooked lasagna noodles (10- x 2-inch/25 x 5 cm pieces)	6

Combine tofu with spinach, two-thirds of Parmesan cheese, parsley and onion powder, oregano, basil and salt.

Spread 1/4 cup (60 mL) of tomato sauce in 9- x 13-inch (3 L) baking dish. Cover with 3 noodles followed by half of tofu mixture, half of grated cheese and 1-1/2 cups (375 mL) tomato sauce. Repeat layers with 3 noodles, remaining tofu, tomato sauce and soy cheese. Sprinkle top with remaining Parmesan. Bake uncovered in a 350°F (180°C) oven for 30 to 40 minutes or until the moisture bubbles on the sides of the pan.

Makes 8 servings

*Sushi,
recipe page 129–30*

Making Sushi

STEP 1: *Spread rice evenly over nori, leaving 1" at top and bottom.*

STEP 2: *Arrange fillings across rice.*

STEP 3: *Moisten top edge with water; roll in jelly roll fashion.*

STEP 4: *Roll tightly with firm pressure, overlapping to seal.*

STEP 5: *Remove sushi mat and place roll seam side down.*

STEP 6: *Moisten knife; slice into 8 equal pieces.*

LEMON GINGER TEMPEH

Tempeh is a traditional Indonesian soyfood with excellent digestibility and protein quality. Like cheese and wines, tempeh is a fermented product and is generally sold frozen to prevent further fermentation. The seasonings most commonly used with tempeh are garlic and ginger, nicely combined here with lemon. Tempeh can be marinated using Tofu Marinade (page 86).

3 tbsp	fresh lemon juice	45 mL
4 tsp	tamari or soy sauce	20 mL
2 tsp	grated ginger	10 mL
1 tsp	chopped garlic	5 mL
1 tsp	canola oil	10 mL
1/2 tsp	powdered onion	2 mL
8 oz	tempeh, sliced in half horizontally	240 g

On a plate, combine lemon juice, tamari, garlic, oil, ginger and onion powders. In lemon juice, marinate tempeh and refrigerate for a minimum of 2 hours, turning occasionally and spooning marinade on top.

Place tempeh under broiler for 4 minutes, turning after 2 minutes, or microwave on High for 1-1/2 minutes or fry in a small amount of oil for about 3 minutes each side or until brown.

Makes 3 servings

Teriyaki Tofu,
recipe page 133, and
Miso Soup,
recipe page 95

PER SERVING

calories 177
protein 15 g
fat 7 g
carbohydrate 16 g
dietary fiber 0.2 g
sodium 365 mg

Good source of:
iron, magnesium, folate, niacin, omega-3 fatty acids
Source of:
calcium, zinc, riboflavin, thiamin, vitamin A

Broiled, or micro-waved without oil:
% Calories from:
protein 32%
fat 35%
carbohydrate 33%

LENTIL DHAL-icious

Dhal is an East Indian word for beans, peas and lentils and the dishes made from them. In this recipe, the "popped" mustard seeds and the other Indian spices, when sautéed in oil, release their fragrant oils and acids into the dhal to create a rich and appetizing dish. Although the dhal is ready to eat when the lentils are soft, best flavor is achieved by simmering on very low heat for 2 hours.

4 tsp	canola oil	20 mL
1 tsp	mustard seeds	5 mL
1/2	onion, diced	1/2
1	garlic clove, minced	1
1 tsp	peeled grated gingerroot	5 mL
1/2 cup	tomato paste	125 mL
1 tsp	each curry powder, garam masala, ground cumin and coriander	5 mL
1 cup	dried lentils	250 mL
2 cups	vegetable stock or water	500 mL
1 cup	each diced carrots and celery	250 mL
1/2 tsp	salt	2 mL

Heat oil over medium heat in large covered pot; add mustard seeds, cover and cook for 1-1/2 minutes or until seeds have popped. Add onion, garlic and ginger; sauté until onion is soft. Stir in tomato paste, curry powder, garam masala, cumin and coriander; sauté for 2 to 3 minutes, stirring frequently. Add lentils and stock; cover; bring to boil then reduce heat and simmer, covered, for 30 minutes. Add carrots, celery and salt; cover and cook another 20 minutes. Adjust seasoning.

Makes 4 servings

MUSHROOM-LENTIL PATTIES

Supermarkets are stocking a great array of veggie burgers for your convenience. Check the refrigerator section, as new products arrive every few months. This home-made rendition, made with lentils and rice, is fresh and full of flavor. Be creative and vary the seasoning, for example with celery seed, cumin or Cajun spice; serve with Light Mushroom Gravy (page 162) or your favorite tomato sauce.

2 cups	water	500 mL
1/2 cup	short-grain brown rice	125 mL
1/2 cup	dried green lentils	125 mL
2 tbsp	vegetable stock or 1 tbsp (15 mL) canola oil	30 mL
1/2	onion, diced	1/2
12	white mushrooms, sliced	12
1/4 cup	fresh bread crumbs	60 mL
3 tbsp	chopped fresh parsley	45 mL
2 tbsp	nutritional yeast	30 mL
1/2 tsp	salt	2 mL
1/4 tsp	each dried thyme, basil and paprika	1 mL
Pinch	black pepper	Pinch
1 tbsp	canola oil	15 mL

Cook water, rice and lentils in covered pot over low heat for 50 minutes. Remove from heat, transfer to bowl and mash with spoon until rice and lentils bind together.

Sauté onion and mushrooms in 2 tbsp (30 mL) stock, adding more stock if necessary, or 1 tbsp (15 mL) oil over medium heat for 5 minutes. Transfer to rice bowl. Stir in bread crumbs, parsley, yeast, salt, thyme, basil, paprika and pepper, mixing well. Form five 4-inch (10 cm) patties. (An easy way to do this is to line 4-inch (10 cm) wide jar lid with clear wrap, fill lid with patty mixture and turn out onto plate.)

Heat olive oil in skillet over medium heat. Cook patties for 2 to 3 minutes or until golden brown or crispy; flip and cook for 2 to 3 minutes.

Makes 5 patties

PER PATTY

calories 248
protein 12 g
fat 5 g
carbohydrate 41 g
dietary fiber 5 g
sodium 332 mg

With oil:
calories 278
fat 8 g

Excellent source of:
iron, magnesium, folate, riboflavin, thiamin
Good source of:
zinc, niacin

% Calories from:
protein 18%
fat 18%
carbohydrate 64%

With optional oil:
% Calories from:
protein 16%
fat 27%
carbohydrate 57%

MUSHROOM RISOTTO

This nourishing version of a classic Italian dish was developed by Chef Michael Fischer. A dear friend and respected colleague, he is talented at developing flavor in vegetarian cuisine. He has created a risotto that is rich and creamy without the traditional use of butter, and enhanced by the addition of nutritional yeast. This recipe can serve as the main part of a meal or as a side dish.

PER SERVING

calories 383
protein 11 g
fat 3 g
carbohydrate 79 g
dietary fiber 4 g
sodium 287 mg

Excellent source of:
magnesium, zinc,
folate, niacin,
riboflavin, thiamin
Good source of:
iron, vitamin E
Source of:
calcium, vitamin A

% Calories from:
protein 11%
fat 7%
carbohydrate 82%

5 cups	water	1.25 L
2 cups	short-grain brown rice	500 mL
2 cups	sliced mushrooms	500 mL
1/2 cup	diced sweet red pepper	125 mL
1	onion, diced	1
2	cloves garlic, diced	2
1/2 tsp	salt	2 mL
1/2 tsp	each dried thyme and rosemary	2 mL
1/8 tsp	black pepper	0.5 mL
1/4 cup	nutritional yeast	60 mL
2 tbsp	chopped fresh parsley	30 mL
2 tsp	tamari or soy sauce (optional)	10 mL

Bring water to boil in large covered pot over high heat. Add rice, mushrooms, red pepper, onion, garlic, salt, thyme, rosemary and pepper. Stir well. Cover and cook for 1 hour over low heat or until water is absorbed by rice.

Remove from heat, stir in yeast, parsley and tamari (if using). Adjust seasoning.

Makes 4 servings

Open-Face Tofu Sandwich

Sandwiches are a mainstay in our culture. Here's a lunchtime favorite. On the following pages you'll find other nutritious choices to give plenty of variety, whether you brown bag it or eat at home. Be creative, add your own combinations and serve them on their own or with soup.

4-6	slices firm tofu, 1/4-inch (5 mm) thick	4-6
2 tsp	low-sodium tamari or soy sauce	10 mL
2 tbsp	mayonnaise (Tofu, page 87 or low-fat)	30 mL
2	slices whole wheat bread	2
8	slices cucumber	8
4	slices tomato	4
Pinch	pepper	Pinch
1/2 cup	alfalfa sprouts (optional)	125 mL

Marinate sliced tofu in tamari on plate for 5 minutes. Warm tofu on medium heat for 1 minute in skillet, turning once, or in microwave. Spread mayonnaise on bread slices. Arrange tofu slices followed by cucumber and tomato slices. Sprinkle with pepper to taste. Garnish with sprouts (if using).

Makes 2 sandwiches

PER SANDWICH

calories 170
protein 11 g
fat 5 g
carbohydrate 23 g
dietary fiber 3 g
sodium 419 mg

Excellent source of:
iron, magnesium
Good source of:
folate, thiamin
Source of:
zinc, calcium, niacin, riboflavin, vitamin E, omega-3 fatty acids

% Calories from:
protein 25%
fat 25%
carbohydrate 50%

Delicious Sandwiches, Vegetarian Style

Go by the bakery and choose multigrain rolls or fresh breads for tomorrow's lunch – or if you're one of the new bread-making enthusiasts, bake your own. Here are some great combinations:

- Yves Veggie Pepperoni or Deli Slices; Polski Ogorki pickle slices; tomato slices; Dijon mustard; mayo
- Crispy Fried Tofu (page 125); tomato slices; lettuce; mayo
- Almond, cashew or peanut butter or tahini; jam, rice syrup or sliced banana
- Gee Whiz Spread (page 52); cucumber slices
- Baked Eggplant (page 139); tomato slices; green pepper slices
- Gooda Cheeze (page 54); alfalfa sprouts; mayo
- Marinated tofu; sprouts
- Debrah's Avocado Dip (page 48); sweet red pepper slices
- Curry Sandwich Spread (page 51); lettuce
- Sun-Dried Tomato Pesto (page 58), canned artichoke slices
- Roasted Garlic and Yam Spread (page 57)
- Hummus (page 55 or commercial); tomato or cucumber slices; chopped Kalamata olives
- Black Bean Hummus (page 49); tomato slices; avocado slices
- Veggieburger or tofuburger, heated; red onion slice; ketchup, relish, mustard; sprouts

These are "sandwiches" from other parts of the world:
- Vegetarian Sushi rolls (page 129–30 or from a deli or Japanese restaurant); soy sauce or tamari; wasabi, pickled ginger
- Salad roll with Peanut Sauce (page 164), Teriyaki Sauce (page 166), barbecue or plum sauce
- International Roll-Ups (page 114–15)

TEN TASTY WAYS TO STUFF YOUR PITA POCKETS

What's better than a two-handed sandwich? Two pita pockets – one in each hand. Try these combinations; mix them up for exciting, ever changing lunch or snack ideas. Kids love 'em and so do adults.

- Debrah's Avocado Dip (page 48), tomato and sprouts
- Black Bean Hummus (page 49) with salsa and quinoa or rice
- Gee Whiz Spread (page 52), diced cucumbers and finely shredded kale or lettuce
- Hummus (page 55), tomato and lettuce
- Hummus (page 55) and Couscous Salad (page 68)
- Lemon-Tahini Dressing (page 83), mashed chick-peas (or falafels from mix), sprouts and diced tomatoes
- Mexican Rice (page 150), lettuce, salsa, soy or Cheddar cheese
- Quinoa Salad (page 75) with lettuce and chick-peas
- Roasted Garlic and Yam Spread (page 57) with diced sweet red, yellow or green pepper
- Sun-Dried Tomato Pesto (page 58) and sprouts

Tofu – An Easy Entrée

Tofu is Asia's #1 fast food. Drawing on the endless variety of Oriental sauces well suited to tofu, we have provided recipes for Teriyaki (page 166) and Peanut Sauce (page 164). The next time you go shopping, look for barbecue, Thai, vegetarian oyster, garlic chili and even more exotic sauces. For any of the options below, you can use firm or extra-firm tofu. For a good source of dietary calcium, select tofu that includes calcium on its package ingredient list.

1	block (12 oz/350 g) firm or extra-firm tofu	1
3 to 6 tbsp	sauce	45-90 mL

Drain tofu and cut into 1/4-inch (5 mm) thick slices. Place tofu slices, touching each other, on lightly oiled or nonstick pan. Spread with sauce. Bake in 350°F (180°C) oven for 20 minutes or until they just begin to brown.

Variation:
Cut tofu into 1 inch cubes (1-1/2 cm), place in pan with sauce and heat through.

CRISPY FRIED TOFU

If you want to introduce tofu to your family or friends, one of the best ways we've ever found is to prepare it as follows with a seasoning salt called Spike, available at all supermarkets. Pan-fried, tofu takes on a crispy southern-fried taste. As a lower fat option these may be baked. Some people like tofu moist, others like it dry, so experiment a little with the cooking time. Crispy Tofu can be used as the protein part of a dinner, as appetizers, as a topping for pizza or in sandwiches.

12 oz	extra-firm tofu	350 g
2 tbsp	light tamari or soy sauce	30 mL
1/4 cup	nutritional yeast	60 mL
1 tsp	Spike or other dehydrated vegetable seasoning	5 mL
1 tbsp	canola oil	15 mL

Cut tofu into 1/4-inch (5 mm) slices. Pour tamari into flat-bottomed bowl. In another bowl, combine yeast with Spike. Dip tofu slices into tamari, then into yeast mixture to coat both sides. Pan-fry coated tofu in a little oil over medium heat for 2 to 3 minutes or until crispy brown. Turn and repeat. Alternatively, place prepared tofu on a lightly oiled or nonstick baking sheet and bake in 350°F (180°C) oven for 10 minutes, until tofu just begins to brown.

Makes 3 servings

PER SERVING

calories 223
protein 22 g
fat 14 g
carbohydrate 8 g
dietary fiber 0.4 g
sodium 438 mg

Excellent source of:
iron, magnesium, folate, riboflavin, thiamin, omega-3 fatty acids
Good source of:
calcium (if using tofu made with calcium), zinc

% Calories from:
protein 36%
fat 51%
carbohydrate 13%

Nutritional Yeast
In choosing nutritional yeast for any of the recipes in this book, we recommend the use of Vegetarian Support Formula Yeast, which was formerly called Red Star T6635+. The use of as little as a teaspoon of this yeast per serving will make the recipe into an excellent source of vitamin B12.

SAVORY BLACK BEAN STEW

This delicious recipe is a splendid example of the balance between protein, fat and carbohydrate recommended in the dietary guidelines (see the first chapter). Served with quinoa or with fresh rolls and Morocc-un-Butter, this iron-rich stew is a very fortifying lunch or supper. It also makes a great combination with rice, rolled up in a soft Mexican tortilla with salsa and fresh cilantro.

1 cup	vegetable stock	250 mL
1 tbsp	canola oil (optional)	15 mL
1 cup	diced celery	250 mL
1 cup	diced carrots	250 mL
1/2	onion, diced	1/2
1	clove garlic, minced	1
3 cups	cooked black turtle beans or black beans	750 mL
1 cup	fresh or canned tomatoes	250 mL
1/4 cup	tomato paste	60 mL
1 tsp	each dried basil, chili powder, ground cumin and ground coriander	5 mL
1/2 tsp	salt	2 mL
1/4 tsp	pepper	1 mL
1/4 cup	chopped fresh cilantro	60 mL
1 tbsp	lime juice	15 mL

Sauté celery, carrots, onion and garlic in 2 tbsp (30 mL) of the stock, adding more stock if necessary, or 1 tbsp (15 mL) oil in large pot over medium heat for 5 minutes.

Stir in remaining stock, beans, tomatoes, paste, basil, chili, cumin, coriander, salt and pepper. Simmer, uncovered, for 20 minutes, adding more stock if needed to just cover beans. Just before serving, stir in fresh cilantro and lime juice. Season to taste.

Makes 5 servings

STUFFED WINTER SQUASH

For some families and groups of friends, getting together to cook is one of the best parts of a celebration. Assembling this stuffing and baked squash can be the central activity for a wonderful day spent with the people you love. Serve it with gravy plus other items from the Thanksgiving and Christmas Menu Selections (page 31). Choose a squash such as hubbard, butternut or acorn. Smaller squashes work too if you can't find a single large one, as referred to in this recipe.

This stuffing can be used to stuff any vegetable. You may want to experiment with different grains such as quinoa, buckwheat or couscous to replace the rice, legumes such as lentils to replace the millet, and cashews or almonds instead of sunflower seeds.

PER SERVING

calories 323
protein 12 g
fat 3 g
carbohydrate 69 g
dietary fiber 10 g
sodium 471 mg

Excellent source of:
folate, thiamin, magnesium, vitamins A and C
Good source of:
iron, niacin, riboflavin
Source of:
calcium, zinc, vitamin E

% Calories from:
protein 14%
fat 8%
carbohydrate 78%

1	winter squash (5 lb/2.5 kg)	1

STUFFING:

1-1/2 cups	cooked brown rice	375 mL
1-1/2 cups	cooked millet	375 mL
2	stalks celery, diced	2
1/2	onion, diced	1/2
2	cloves garlic, minced	2
1 cup	corn kernels, fresh, canned or frozen	250 mL
1/2 cup	diced sweet red pepper	125 mL
1/2 cup	sunflower seeds (optional)	125 mL
1/4 cup	chopped fresh parsley	60 mL
1 tsp	each dried oregano and thyme	5 mL
1/2 tsp	each sage and celery seed	2 mL
2-3 tbsp	tamari or soy sauce	30-45 mL
1/4-1/2 tsp	salt	1-2 mL
1/8 tsp	pepper	0.5 mL

Squash: Pierce top of squash with sharp knife at 45° angle. Pushing knife blade away from your body, rotate blade around top of squash and remove cone-shaped top piece. Remove any fibrous material from top and set top aside. Remove seeds and pulp from cavity of squash using soup spoon. Set squash and top on baking pan in 350°F (180°C) oven and bake for 30 minutes.

Remove squash and lid from oven and set aside to cool for 15 minutes.

Stuffing: Combine rice and millet in large bowl and set aside to cool.

Sauté celery, onion and garlic in 2 tbsp (30 mL) water in skillet, adding more water if necessary, over medium heat for 3 to 5 minutes or until onions are soft. Transfer to grains bowl along with corn, red pepper, sunflower seeds (if using), parsley, oregano, thyme, sage, celery seeds, tamari, salt and pepper. Stir together and adjust seasoning.

Spoon stuffing into cavity of squash until almost full.

Set lid in place, return squash to pie plate and bake in 350°F (180°C) oven for 45 to 60 minutes or until toothpick can be inserted easily into squash.

If you have leftover stuffing, place in loaf pan, sprinkle with 2 to 3 tbsp (30 to 45 mL) of stock or water, cover, and heat through for last 20 minutes of squash cooking time.

Remove squash from oven and place on warm serving platter. Slice into wedges.

Makes 5 cups (1.25 L) stuffing, 5 hearty servings

SUSHI

It's fun to make this recipe with someone else. In fact, Joseph and Debrah became acquainted making sushi and discovered their love for each other. Sushi is rolled using a bamboo sushi mat. The mat helps keep the pressure uniform during the rolling process and keeps the nori seaweed from being torn. Bamboo mats, along with the other less familiar ingredients in this recipe, are available from Oriental stores. You may use the ingredients listed below, those listed in the variation (shown in the photo) or use your own ideas.

2 cups	water	500 mL
1 cup	brown rice	250 mL
1/4 tsp	salt (optional)	15 mL
2 tbsp	rice vinegar	30 mL
1 tbsp	Sucanat or sugar	15 mL
3	sheets nori seaweed	3
3 tbsp	mayonnaise (tofu or low-fat)	45 mL
1-1/2 cups	grated carrots	375 mL
6	slices avocado	6
6	cucumber matchsticks, 2 inches (5 cm) long	6
2	lettuce leaves, cut into 1/2-inch (1 cm) wide strips	2
1 tbsp	thinly sliced pickled ginger	15 mL
1-1/2 tsp	Gomasio (page 59)	7 mL

PER ROLL (8 PIECES)

calories 338
protein 8 g
fat 7 g
carbohydrate 61 g
dietary fiber 5 g
sodium 141 mg (not including sodium in dipping tamari)

Excellent source of:
magnesium, thiamin, vitamin A
Good source of:
iron, zinc, folate, niacin, vitamin E
Source of:
calcium, riboflavin

% Calories from:
protein 10%
fat 19%
carbohydrate 72%

1 tsp	wasabi horseradish powder	5 mL
	Water	
2 tbsp	pickled ginger	30 mL
2 tbsp	tamari or soy sauce	30 mL

Bring water with salt (if using) to boil. Add rice, cover, reduce heat and simmer for 45 minutes. In small bowl combine rice vinegar and Sucanat. Drizzle vinegar mixture over cooked rice, mixing with fork. Set aside to cool completely before assembling rolls.

Set out all ingredients needed for rolls on counter. Lay down sheet of nori seaweed on bamboo sushi mat. Spoon 3/4 cup (175 mL) rice over nori sheet as shown in Step 2 of Making Sushi photo sequence, leaving 1-inch (2.5 cm) border at bottom and top and spooning rice out to right and left edges. Spread one-third of the mayonnaise over rice in single strip near bottom of nori sheet. Layer one-third of carrots, avocado, cucumber, lettuce, ginger and Gomasio over mayonnaise. Dip index finger into bowl of water and moisten top edge of nori sheet to ensure seal. Using both hands and firm pressure, lift mat and roll like jelly roll until sushi roll is formed. Repeat until three rolls have been assembled.

Place roll on cutting board, seam side down; trim ends of any food that squeezed out during rolling. Cut each roll into 8 equal slices using serrated knife; arrange on platter.

In small bowl, mix wasabi powder with a few drops of water, gradually adding more water until smooth paste forms. Place wasabi paste on platter along with pickled ginger. Serve with small bowl of tamari.

Makes 24 pieces, 3 entrées or 6 appetizer-size servings

SWEET AND SOUR TOFU

Since vinegar made from rice is less acidic than when made from fruit, its use in this stir-fry creates a dish that is more smooth than sharp. This allows a smaller amount of sweetener to be added with the effect that the inherent sweetness from the vegetables isn't masked. Best served on a bed of rice, this recipe on its own will easily feed two hungry adults, or four if other items are included in the meal.

2 tbsp	vegetable stock or water or 1 tbsp (15 mL) canola oil	30 mL
1 cup	diced onion	250 mL
1 cup	diagonally sliced carrots	250 mL
1 cup	each diced sweet green and red pepper	250 mL
1 tbsp	minced garlic	15 mL
1 tbsp	peeled grated gingerroot	15 mL
3/4 cup	pineapple juice	175 mL
1/4 cup	Sucanat or brown sugar	60 mL
1/4 cup	rice vinegar	60 mL
2 tsp	cornstarch	10 mL
1 cup	diced firm tofu	250 mL
1 tbsp	chopped fresh parsley	15 mL

Sauté onions, carrots, peppers, garlic and ginger in 2 tbsp (30 mL) stock, adding more stock if necessary, or 1 tbsp (15 mL) oil in skillet over medium heat for 5 minutes. Mix together pineapple juice, sugar, vinegar and cornstarch and add to skillet along with tofu, stirring constantly until thickened. Simmer, covered, for 3 minutes. Garnish with parsley.

Makes 4 servings

PER SERVING

calories 176
protein 7 g
fat 3 g
carbohydrate 32 g
dietary fiber 4 g
sodium 52 mg

With oil:
calories 206
fat 7 g

Excellent source of:
iron, magnesium,
vitamins A, C and E
Good source of: folate
Source of:
calcium, zinc,
riboflavin, thiamin,
omega-3 fatty acids

% *Calories from*:
protein 15%
fat 16%
carbohydrate 69%

With oil:
% *Calories from*:
protein 13%
fat 28%
carbohydrate 59%

SZECHUAN VEGETABLES OVER BUCKWHEAT NOODLES

Szechuan province in western China is famous for the spicy hot food that has been developed using combinations of chili and other spices. This dish is spiced mildly; you can make it hotter by increasing the amounts of chili paste and ginger. Buckwheat is in fact not a wheat but is the seed of a plant in the rhubarb family.

PER SERVING

calories 267
protein 11 g
fat 7 g
carbohydrate 44 g
dietary fiber 7 g
sodium 464 mg

Excellent source of:
magnesium, iron, folate, riboflavin, vitamins A, C and E
Good source of:
niacin, thiamin, omega-3 fatty acids
Source of:
calcium, zinc

% Calories from:
protein 15%
fat 22%
carbohydrate 63%

8 oz	buckwheat noodles	240 g
1 tbsp	canola oil	15 mL
1 cup	sliced mushrooms	250 mL
1	onion, chopped in 1/2-inch (1 cm) pieces	1
2	cloves garlic, minced	2
1–2 tsp	peeled grated gingerroot	5–10 mL
1 cup	sliced carrots	250 mL
1 cup	broccoli florets	250 mL
1 cup	water	250 mL
1/4 cup	black bean sauce	60 mL
1 tbsp	cornstarch	15 mL
1/4–1/2 tsp	fresh chili paste	1–2 mL
2 tsp	tamari or soy sauce	10 mL
2 cups	bean sprouts	500 mL
1 cup	sliced snow peas	250 mL
2 tbsp	chopped fresh cilantro	30 mL

Cook noodles in boiling water for 5–8 minutes or until tender. Stir gently to keep from sticking. Meanwhile, in wok, sauté mushrooms, onion, garlic and ginger in oil over medium heat for 5 minutes. Stir in carrots and broccoli; cook for 3 to 5 minutes or until vegetables are tender-crisp. In small bowl combine water, black bean sauce, cornstarch, chili paste and tamari. Reduce heat to low; stir cornstarch mixture into wok along with bean sprouts and snow peas.

Cover and cook for 2 to 3 minutes after liquid has thickened. Stir once or twice. Garnish with cilantro.

Makes 3 servings

TERIYAKI TOFU

Striking a balance between salty and sweet, this dish includes an abundance of vegetables. Served over a bed of whole grain rice or your favorite noodles, it makes a fully satisfying, attractive meal.

2 tbsp	vegetable stock or 1 tbsp (15 mL) canola oil	30 mL
1 cup	each diced carrots and daikon radish	250 mL
1/2	onion, diced	1/2
1	clove garlic, minced	1
1 tsp	peeled grated gingerroot	5 mL
1 cup	each diced sweet red and green peppers	250 mL
1 cup	diced firm tofu	250 mL
1 cup	Teriyaki Sauce (page 166)	250 mL
1–2 tbsp	chopped fresh cilantro	15–30 mL

In large skillet, sauté carrots, radish, onion, garlic and ginger in 2 tbsp (30 mL) stock, adding more stock if necessary, or 1 tbsp (15 mL) oil over medium heat for 5 minutes. Stir in peppers and tofu; sauté for 3 minutes. Pour in Teriyaki Sauce; cover and simmer for 2 to 3 minutes.

Garnish with cilantro.

Makes 4 servings

PER SERVING

calories 203
protein 13 g
fat 6 g
carbohydrate 28 g
dietary fiber 3 g
sodium 586 mg

With oil:
calories 247
fat 9 g

Excellent source of:
iron, magnesium,
vitamins A and C
Good source of:
calcium, folate,
omega-3 fatty acids
Source of:
zinc, riboflavin,
thiamin

% Calories from:
protein 24%
fat 24%
carbohydrate 52%

With oil:
% Calories from:
protein 20%
fat 32%
carbohydrate 48%

VEGGIE PEPPERONI PIZZA

Pizza can be a wonderful balance of nutritious foods: look at all the vitamins and minerals in this one! It can be served as a quick and easy meal or snack for children of all ages. For adults, be creative and use more exotic ingredients like artichokes, soaked sun-dried tomatoes or capers.

PER PIZZA

calories 156
protein 6 g
fat 2 g
carbohydrate 20 g
dietary fiber 3 g
sodium 670 mg

Good source of:
iron
Source of:
calcium, magnesium,
zinc, folate, niacin,
riboflavin, thiamin,
vitamins A and E

% Calories from:
protein 20%
fat 14%
carbohydrate 66%

4	pita bread (each 6 in/15 cm) or pizza shells	4
1 cup	tomato sauce	250 mL
8	slices veggie pepperoni, quartered	8
12	thin slices tomato	12
1/2	red onion, sliced thinly	1/2
1/2	sweet green pepper, sliced thinly	1/2
4-6	mushrooms, sliced	4-6
8	black olives, sliced	8
1/4 cup	sliced green onions	60 mL
1/4 cup	Veganrella or Parmesan cheese	60 mL
4 tsp	chopped fresh basil	20 mL

Cover pita bread with tomato sauce. Evenly distribute pepperoni followed by tomato slices, onion, green pepper and mushrooms. Garnish with olives and green onions, then sprinkle with cheese. Place on a lightly oiled pan and bake in 375°F (190°C) oven for 10 to 12 minutes or until browned. Top with fresh basil and cut each pizza in quarters.

Makes 4 pizzas

VEGETABLE KABOBS

The assortment of vegetables that make up these kabobs are very colorful and the Tofu Marinade makes them burst with flavor. Assemble the kabobs before a picnic or beach barbecue. Serve on a bed of rice or in a pita pocket with Cucumber Dressing (page 80).

1	pkg (10 oz/300 g) firm tofu	1
	Tofu Marinade (page 86)	
16	small mushrooms	16
1	sweet red bell pepper	1
1	zucchini	1
8	cherry tomatoes	8

Cut tofu into 3/4-inch (2 cm) cubes. Cover with Tofu Marinade and refrigerate for 4 to 6 hours.

Cut bell pepper and zucchini into same size pieces as tofu. (You should have 16 pieces each of peppers and zucchini.)

Starting and ending with mushrooms, thread vegetables onto eight 10-inch (25 cm) bamboo skewers. A possible sequence is mushroom, red pepper, tofu, zucchini, tofu, cherry tomato, tofu, zucchini, tofu, red pepper, mushroom.

Grill skewers or place on baking sheet 6 inches (15 mL) under broiler for 10 minutes, turning and basting occasionally with marinade.

Makes 4 servings

ZUCCHINI STUFFED WITH LENTILS AND BULGUR

Zucchini is one of the most abundant of the summer squashes and it can be easily grown in the garden or on a sunny balcony. This lentil, bulgur and dill stuffing can also be used to fill other vegetables such as sweet peppers, eggplant, squash or tomatoes.

1/2 cup	dry lentils	125 mL
1-1/2 cups	water	375 mL
1/2	small onion, diced	1/2
1	clove garlic, minced	1
1/4 cup	bulgur	60 mL
1/2 cup	tomato juice	125 mL
2	zucchini, each 8" (20 cm) x 2-1/2" (6 cm)	2
2 tbsp	parsley, chopped	30 mL
2 tbsp	lemon juice	30 mL
3/4 tsp	dill weed	4 mL
1/4 tsp	salt	1 mL
Pinch	black pepper	Pinch

Bring lentils, water, onions and garlic to a boil in covered pot, reduce heat and simmer for 45 minutes. Heat tomato juice, pour over bulgur in bowl and let soak for 15 minutes.

Halve zucchinis lengthwise and, using teaspoon, scoop out and discard pulp starting 1 inch (2.5 cm) from either end, leaving shell 1/2 inch (2.5 cm) thick.

To make stuffing, combine lentil mixture, soaked bulgur, parsley, lemon juice, dill weed, salt and pepper. Mix well and adjust seasoning.

Place stuffing in cavity of zucchinis, set on baking sheet and bake at 350°F (180°C) for 20-30 minutes or until the zucchini is soft.

Makes 4 servings

SIDE DISHES

Baked Potato and Fixings

What can you do with a baked potato if you don't load it up with butter and sour cream? Here are a wealth of new ideas to brighten up your dinner table. In fact, with a variety of these toppings, you can build a meal around baked potatoes by adding soup or salad. Potatoes bake very well without oil; however, coating with a minimal amount will soften the skin, which some people prefer.

| 1 | russet or similar baking potato, washed | 1 |
| 1/4 tsp | canola oil (optional) | 1 mL |

Rub oil (if using) over potato.

Oven method:

Pierce potato 3 to 4 times with fork, place in 375°F (190°C) oven and bake for about 45 minutes or until soft when skewer is inserted into potato.

Microwave method:

Heat 1 potato on High for about 5 minutes, depending on size of potato.

Cut X on top of potato and top with any of the following suggestions.

Low-calorie toppings:

- Cucumber Dill Dressing (page 80)
- Salsa
- Salt and freshly cracked pepper
- Diced red pepper, tomato, cucumber
- Dulse or kelp powder/flakes
- Fresh chopped herbs (parsley, basil)
- Gomasio (page 59)
- Miso, thinned with a little water
- Veggie (soy) bacon bits
- Nutritional yeast

Creamy smooth Toppings

- Caesar Dressing (page 67)
- Debrah's Avocado Dip (page 48)
- Extra virgin olive oil
- Flax seed oil
- Grated tofu cheese
- Lemon Tahini Dressing (page 183)
- Morocc-un Butter (page 56)
- Sun-dried Tomato Pesto (page 58)

BAKED EGGPLANT

This recipe is similar to the Crispy Fried Tofu (page 125) in that it incorporates seasoned nutritional yeast as the coating for the eggplant. Since eggplant is porous it absorbs liquid or oil quite readily. Dredge the sliced eggplant *very* briefly – that is, do not let it sit in the soy sauce, otherwise it will be too salty. Any combination of Middle Eastern spices with the yeast work well with eggplant: cumin, paprika, coriander, cayenne, garlic and turmeric. Serve this vegetable on its own or with a tomato sauce.

1	eggplant, cut in 1/2-inch (1 cm) thick slices	1	
2 tbsp	light tamari or soy sauce	30 mL	
1/3 cup	nutritional yeast	75 mL	
1 tsp	ground cumin, garlic powder, paprika or combination	5 mL	

Arrange on counter sliced eggplant, flat-bottomed bowl containing tamari, another bowl containing yeast mixed with seasonings, and nonstick or lightly oiled baking sheet. Dip eggplant slices into tamari and then into seasoned yeast to coat both sides. Place slices on baking sheet. Bake in 350°F (180°C) oven for 25 minutes.

For a Kentucky-fried taste, sauté coated slices in batches over medium heat in a little oil until crispy brown; turn and brown second side. Add more oil when necessary.

Makes 4 servings

PER SERVING

calories 67
protein 6 g
fat 1 g
carbohydrate 12 g
dietary fiber 3 g
sodium 275 mg

Excellent source of:
folate, riboflavin, thiamin, vitamins C and B12
Good source of:
zinc
Source of:
iron, magnesium, niacin

Baked:
% Calories from:
protein 30%
fat 9%
carbohydrate 61%

Fried:
Much higher in fat – eggplant can soak up a lot of oil!

Bok Choy, Mushrooms and Ginger

If you look at the Vegetarian Food Guide in chapter 1, you'll see that bok choy is a calcium-rich food. This combination of Oriental-style glazed vegetables makes an excellent side dish.

Per serving

calories 77
protein 3 g
fat 5 g
carbohydrate 7 g
dietary fiber 2 g
sodium 253 mg

Excellent source of:
folate, vitamin C
Good source of:
vitamin A

Source of:
calcium, iron,
magnesium, niacin,
riboflavin, thiamin,
omega-3 fatty acids

% Calories from:
protein 12%
fat 56%
carbohydrate 32%

4 tsp	canola oil	20 mL
2 cups	sliced mushrooms	500 mL
1/2	onion, cut in half then sliced lengthwise	1/2
1	clove garlic, minced	1
2 tsp	peeled, minced gingerroot	10 mL
4 cups	sliced bok choy	1 L
1/4 cup	diagonally sliced green onions	60 mL
1/2 cup	water	125 mL
1 1/2 tsp	cornstarch	7 mL
1 tbsp	tamari or soy sauce	15 mL
1/4 tsp	toasted sesame oil	1 mL
1 tbsp	chopped fresh cilantro or parsley	15 mL

In wok or large skillet, sauté mushrooms, onion, garlic and ginger in oil over medium-high heat for 5 minutes. Stir in bok choy and green onions; cook for 2 to 3 minutes. In small bowl, combine water, cornstarch, tamari and sesame oil. Reduce heat to medium-low, stir in cornstarch mixture, cover and cook, stirring 2 or 3 times, until liquid has thickened and glazed vegetables. Garnish with cilantro or parsley.

Makes 4 servings

CARROTS AND BROCCOLI WITH HIJIKI

Hijiki, also known as hiziki, is a black seaweed rich in trace minerals. In this stir-fry it contrasts visually with the bright green broccoli and the deep orange carrots. Toasted sesame oil brings a rich nutty flavor that blends exceptionally well with hijiki. Rice syrup is a mild, subtle sweetener that takes the edge off the strong-tasting hijiki.

PER SERVING

calories 72
protein 3 g
fat 1 g
carbohydrate 16 g
dietary fiber 4 g
sodium 131 mg

With canola oil:
calories 102
fat 4 g

Excellent source of:
vitamins A and C
Good source of:
folate
Source of:
calcium, iron, magnesium, riboflavin, thiamin and vitamin E

% Calories from:
protein 14%
fat 7%
carbohydrate 79%

With canola oil:
% Calories from:
protein 10%
fat 33%
carbohydrate 57%

2 tsp	dried hijiki seaweed	10 mL
2 tbsp	vegetable stock or 1 tbsp (15 mL) canola oil	30 mL
1/4 tsp	toasted sesame oil	1 mL
1	red onion, chopped	1
1	clove garlic, minced	1
1 tsp	peeled grated gingerroot	5 mL
1-1/2 cups	sliced carrots	375 mL
1-1/2 cups	broccoli florets	375 mL
1 tsp	tamari or soy sauce	5 mL
1 tbsp	rice syrup or honey	15 mL

Soak hijiki in bowl of water for at least 15 minutes. Rinse under cold water.

In large skillet, sauté onion, garlic and ginger in 2 tbsp (30 mL) stock, adding more stock if necessary, or 1 tbsp (15 mL) canola and 1/4 tsp (1 mL) sesame oil over medium heat for 5 minutes or until onions are soft. Add carrots and broccoli; sauté for 3 minutes.

Stir in rinsed hijiki, tamari and sweetener.

Makes 4 servings

CAULIFLOWER AND YAM

Powdered spices such as curry powder and mustard seeds are heated in a small amount of oil to release their volatile oils, making this dish fragrant and flavorful.

Per serving

calories 170
protein 3 g
fat 5 g
carbohydrate 29 g
dietary fiber 4 g
sodium 163 mg

Excellent source of:
vitamins A, C and E
Good source of:
folate
Source of:
iron, magnesium, zinc,
riboflavin, thiamin

% Calories from:
protein 7%
fat 27%
carbohydrate 66%

4 tsp	canola oil	20 mL
I tsp	mustard seeds	5 mL
1/2	onion, sliced	1/2
I tsp	curry powder	5 mL
I tsp	coriander seeds, crushed, or 1/2 tsp (2 mL) ground coriander	5 mL
2 cups	cauliflower florets, cut into bite-size pieces	500 mL
2 cups	diced yams	500 mL
3/4 cup	water	175 mL
1/4 tsp	salt	1 mL

Heat mustard seeds in oil over medium heat in covered pot or skillet. As soon as seeds have popped (1-2 minutes), stir in onion, curry powder and coriander seeds; sauté for 3 to 4 minutes. Stir in cauliflower, yams, water and salt, stirring well. Cover and simmer for 15 minutes or until vegetables are tender-crisp.

Makes 4 servings

CORN WITH RED PEPPERS

What a pleasure it is when the season for fresh corn arrives! This gold and red vegetable combination goes well with Savory Black Bean Stew (page 126) and either Quinoa Salad (page 75) or a steaming plate of rice. To remove the kernels of corn from the ear, slice off the stem and place the ear of corn, stem end down, on a damp cloth to avoid slipping. Remove kernels by slicing from top to bottom all around the ear. One large ear will produce about 1 cup (250 mL) of corn.

2 tbsp	vegetable stock or water	30 mL
1 tbsp	canola oil (optional)	15 mL
1/2	red onion, chopped	1/2
1	clove garlic, minced	1
3 cups	fresh, canned or frozen corn kernels	750 mL
1/3 cup	diced sweet red pepper	75 mL
1/8 tsp	salt	0.5 mL
Pinch	pepper	Pinch

Sauté onion and garlic in 2 tbsp (30 mL) stock, adding more if necessary, or in 1 tbsp (15 mL) oil over medium heat for 3 to 5 minutes or until onions are soft. Add corn, sweet pepper, salt and pepper, cover and cook for 5 minutes. Adjust seasoning.

Makes 4 servings

PER SERVING

calories 108
protein 4 g
fat 0.1 g
carbohydrate 27 g
dietary fiber 3 g
sodium 73 mg

With oil:
calories 162
fat 4 g

Excellent source of:
vitamin C
Source of:
magnesium, folate,
riboflavin, thiamin,
vitamin A

% *Calories from:*
protein 13%
fat 1%
carbohydrate 86%

With oil:
% *Calories from:*
protein 10%
fat 22%
carbohydrate 68%

DIJON SCALLOPED POTATOES

Scalloped potatoes are generally made with loads of milk, cream and butter. This version is dairy-free and the fat content has been kept to a minimum. Miso combined with Dijon mustard give the dish a distinctly different appeal. Use unpeeled potatoes to retain the fiber and nutritional value that reside in the skin.

PER SERVING

calories 174
protein 4 g
fat 5 g
carbohydrate 29 g
dietary fiber 3 g
sodium 300 mg

Source of:
iron, magnesium, zinc, folate, niacin, riboflavin, thiamin

% Calories from:
protein 8%
fat 27%
carbohydrate 65%

1/4 cup	unbleached or all-purpose flour	60 mL
2 tbsp	oil	30 mL
2 cups	vegetable stock	500 mL
2 tbsp	miso	30 mL
1 tbsp	Dijon mustard	15 mL
1/8 tsp	pepper	0.5 mL
4	potatoes (unpeeled)	4
1/2	red onion	1/2
2 tbsp	bread crumbs	30 mL

In saucepan over medium heat, combine flour and oil; cook for 3 minutes, stirring frequently to prevent flour from burning. Set aside to cool for 3 minutes. Return to heat and stir continuously while gradually pouring stock into saucepan. Bring to boil, reduce heat and cook for 10 minutes, stirring occasionally.

Meanwhile, in small bowl, combine miso, mustard and pepper, mixing until miso is dissolved.

Cut 2 potatoes into 1/4-inch (5 mm) slices and layer in lightly oiled 8-inch (2 L) square baking dish. Thinly slice onion and spread over potatoes. Slice remaining 2 potatoes and spread over onions.

When sauce is cooked, remove from heat, stir in miso mixture and adjust seasoning. Pour over potatoes, cover with foil and cook in 375°F (190°C) oven for 30 minutes. Remove foil, sprinkle evenly with bread crumbs and return to oven, uncovered, for 20 minutes or until potatoes are cooked.

Makes 6 servings

GREEN BEANS WITH BLACK BEANS

The combination of green beans, which are native to South America and common to North America, with black bean sauce gives the dish an Oriental flavor.

2 tsp	canola oil	10 mL
1/2	onion, chopped	1/2
1	clove garlic, minced	1
2 cups	chopped canned (drained) or fresh tomatoes	500 mL
2 cups	diagonally sliced green beans	500 mL
2 tbsp	black bean sauce	30 mL
2 tsp	slivered almonds or sesame seeds (optional)	10 mL

Sauté onion and garlic in 3 tbsp (45 mL) of liquid from tomatoes or 2 tsp (10 mL) canola oil in skillet over medium heat for 3 to 5 minutes or until onions are softened. Add tomatoes and continue cooking for 5 minutes to reduce liquid from tomatoes.

Add green beans, and continue cooking for 3 to 4 minutes until beans are tender-crisp. Stir in black bean sauce; garnish with almonds or sesame seeds.

Makes 4 servings

PER SERVING

calories 85
protein 3 g
fat 2 g
carbohydrate 15 g
dietary fiber 4 g
sodium 337 mg

With oil and garnish:
calories 126
fat 7

Excellent source of:
vitamin C
Good source of:
folate, magnesium
Source of:
calcium, iron, zinc, niacin, riboflavin, thiamin, vitamins A and E

Without garnish:
% Calories from:
protein 14%
fat 20%
carbohydrate 66%

With oil and garnish:
% Calories from:
protein 9%
fat 55%
carbohydrate 36%

GREENS WITH TOMATOES AND GARLIC

This exceptional nutritionally well-balanced dish can be the backbone of your calcium-rich recipes. The vitamin C in the tomatoes greatly helps our bodies absorb the iron in fresh kale. Furthermore, it tastes very good indeed!

PER SERVING

calories 102
protein 6 g
fat 1 g
carbohydrate 21 g
dietary fiber 5 g
sodium 204 mg

Excellent source of:
magnesium, vitamins A, C and E
Good source of:
calcium, iron, folate, riboflavin, thiamin
Source of:
zinc, niacin

% Calories from:
protein 19%
fat 11%
carbohydrate 70%

2 cups	chopped fresh or canned (drained) tomatoes	500 mL
1	clove garlic, minced	1
1/2 tsp	each dried basil and oregano	2 mL
8 cups	sliced kale greens	2 L
1/4 tsp	salt	1 mL
Pinch	pepper	Pinch

In skillet, sauté tomatoes, garlic, basil and oregano over medium heat until most of the liquid from tomatoes has evaporated, about 3 to 5 minutes.

Meanwhile, remove stems from kale; chop kale leaves into bite-size pieces.

Add kale greens, salt and pepper to skillet; cover and cook for 2 minutes. Adjust seasoning.

Makes 4 servings

KALE AND RED PEPPER RING

The deep green kale tossed with bright red peppers resembles a holly wreath when presented in a circle on a plate. This simple yet elegant dish is perfect for the holiday season and adds color and a festive touch any time in the year.

6 cups	thinly sliced kale	1.5 L
1/4 cup	diced sweet red pepper	60 mL
2 tbsp	flaxseed oil (optional)	30 mL
1 tbsp	balsamic vinegar	15 mL
1 tbsp	tamari	15 mL
1 tbsp	sesame seeds (optional)	15 mL

Place kale in steamer, sprinkle with red pepper. Cover and steam over medium-high heat until the peppers are tender-crisp. Drain.

Combine flaxseed oil (if using), vinegar, tamari and sesame seeds (if using) in a bowl large enough to hold kale. Toss kale and peppers in vinegar mixture and place on warm platter. Create wreath shape by pushing kale toward edges of platter, leaving open space in center.

Makes 4 servings

PER SERVING

calories 55
protein 4 g
fat 1 g
carbohydrate 11 g
dietary fiber 3 g
sodium 246 mg

With oil and seeds:
calories 132
fat 9 g

Excellent source of:
vitamins A, C and E
(and omega-3 fatty
acids with flaxseed
oil)
Good source of:
magnesium
Source of:
calcium, iron, zinc,
folate, niacin,
riboflavin, thiamin

% Calories from:
protein 23%
fat 10%
carbohydrate 67%

With oil and seeds:
% Calories from:
protein 13%
fat 55%
carbohydrate 32%

LEMON ROASTED POTATOES

The Greeks make spectacular but high-fat roasted potatoes using seasonings, lemon and olive oil. This version keeps the lemon and herb flavor but greatly reduces the oil and salt.

Per serving

calories 155
protein 3 g
fat 2 g
carbohydrate 31 g
dietary fiber 3 g
sodium 188 mg

Excellent source of:
vitamin C (Yes – even roasted!)
Source of:
iron, magnesium, folate, niacin, thiamin

% Calories from:
protein 7%
fat 14%
carbohydrate 79%

6	potatoes (unpeeled)	6
2 tbsp	lemon juice	30 mL
1 tbsp	extra-virgin olive oil	15 mL
2 tbsp	chopped fresh parsley	30 mL
1 tsp	dried basil	5 mL
1/2 tsp	dried oregano	2 mL
1/2 tsp	salt	2 mL
1/4 tsp	pepper	1 mL

Wash potatoes and cut each into 8. Toss in large bowl with lemon juice, olive oil, parsley, basil, oregano, salt and pepper.

Transfer to 13- x 9-inch (3 L) baking dish and bake, uncovered, in 350°F (180°C) oven for 30 minutes or until soft.

Makes 6 servings

*Fruit Shakes,
recipe page 36*

MASHED POTATOES

Few foods are as comforting as creamy mashed potatoes. Fresh herbs and spices, such as the coriander found in this recipe, can add interesting flavor combinations. As in the Dijon Scalloped Potatoes, (page 144) and the Potato Dill Salad (page 74) skins are left on for added nutritional value.

4	potatoes (unpeeled)	4
1/2 cup	soy or dairy milk	125 mL
2 tbsp	chopped fresh parsley	30 mL
1 tbsp	extra-virgin olive oil (optional)	15 mL
1/2 tsp	coriander seeds, crushed	2 mL
1/4 tsp	salt	1 mL
Pinch	white pepper	Pinch
1 tbsp	chopped green onions	15 mL

PER SERVING

calories 128
protein 3 g
fat 1 g
carbohydrate 28 g
dietary fiber 2 g
sodium 145 mg

With oil:
calories 158
fat 4 g

Source of:
iron, magnesium,
folate, niacin, thiamin

% Calories from:
protein 10%
fat 5%
carbohydrate 85%

With oil:
% Calories from:
protein 8%
fat 23%
carbohydrate 69%

Quarter potatoes and cook in pot of boiling water for 15 to 20 minutes or until tender. Drain water from pot and reserve for vegetable stock. Add milk, parsley, olive oil (if using), coriander, salt and pepper, and mash well by hand or with an electric beater. Blend in green onions and adjust seasoning.

Makes 4 servings

Blueberry Mince Tarts,
recipe page 178–79

MEXICAN RICE

This rice turns out very moist due to the tomatoes, and rich in flavor from the peppers, herbs and spices. It is a great accompaniment to Savory Black Beans (page 126) or Chili with Textured Soy Protein (page 108).

2 cups	vegetable stock	500 mL
2 tsp	canola oil (optional)	10 mL
1/2	small onion, diced	1/2
1	clove garlic, minced	1
2 cups	chopped fresh or canned tomatoes	500 mL
1 cup	brown rice	250 mL
1/4 cup	each diced sweet red and green pepper	60 mL
1/2 tsp	each dried oregano, ground cumin and chili powder	2 mL
1/4 tsp	salt	1 mL
Pinch	pepper	Pinch

In pot, sauté onion and garlic in 2 tbsp (30 mL) of the stock, adding more stock if necessary, or 2 tsp (10 mL) oil over medium heat for 5 minutes or until onion is soft. Add remaining stock, tomatoes, rice, red and green peppers, oregano, cumin, chili powder, salt and pepper. Cover, reduce heat and cook for 45 minutes.

Makes 4 servings

POTATO SUBJI

India has a tradition of vegetarian cuisine with roots in antiquity. As a consequence its food combinations have a great deal to offer the West in depth, color, richness and variety. An example is found here in one of the tastiest ways ever invented to eat potatoes!

2 tbsp	canola oil	30 mL
1 tbsp	yellow mustard seeds	15 mL
1	onion, diced	1
2 tsp	turmeric	10 mL
4	potatoes cut in 1/2-inch (1 cm) cubes	4
1/4 cup	water (more if necessary)	60 mL
1 tsp	salt	5 mL

PER SERVING

calories 190
protein 4 g
fat 4 g
carbohydrate 35 g
dietary fiber 4 g
sodium 544 mg

Excellent source of:
vitamin C
Good source of:
iron, magnesium
Source of:
zinc, folate, niacin,
thiamin

% Calories from:
protein 8%
fat 21%
carbohydrate 71%

Heat mustard seeds in oil over medium heat in pan. Once seeds begin to pop, cover pan with lid and wait until they've popped, about 1 1/2 minutes. Add onion and turmeric; sauté for 3 to 5 minutes or until onion is soft.

Stir in potatoes, water and salt. Cover and simmer for 20 minutes or until potatoes are tender, adding more water if necessary to prevent potatoes from drying out.

Makes 4 servings

Seasoned Potato Wedges

These wedges are a delicious alternative to French fries. Easy to prepare, they can be served alone or with Peanut Sauce (page 164), Cucumber Dill Dressing (page 80) or other favorite dipping sauces. Experiment with different herb and spice combinations in the yeast mixture. Any leftover yeast mixture can be sprinkled over casseroles, salad or popcorn.

Per serving

calories 184
protein 10 g
fat 1 g
carbohydrate 37 g
dietary fiber 4 g
sodium 389 mg

Excellent source of:
magnesium, folate,
riboflavin, thiamin
Good source of:
iron, zinc
Source of:
niacin, vitamin A

% Calories from:
protein 19%
fat 6%
carbohydrate 75%

3	russet potatoes	3
1/4 cup	plain soy or cow's milk	60 mL
1/2 tsp	salt	2 mL
1/3 cup	nutritional yeast	75 mL
2 tsp	onion powder	10 mL
2 tsp	chili powder	10 mL
3/4 tsp	garlic powder	4 mL
1/4 tsp	pepper	1 mL

Cut each potato in half lengthwise; cut each half lengthwise into thirds.

Pour milk and salt into flat-bottomed bowl and stir to dissolve salt.

Sprinkle yeast onto plate; stir in onion, chili and garlic powders and pepper.

Dip potatoes into milk then into yeast mixture until coated. Arrange on nonstick baking sheet and bake for 30 minutes in 400°F (200°C) oven.

Makes 3 servings

Baking Variation:

For crispy fries, lightly oil a baking sheet and arrange potatoes cut side down. Bake in 400°F (200°C) oven for 15 minutes. Using fork or metal tongs, turn wedges and bake for another 15 minutes.

RED CABBAGE WITH WALNUTS

Here's a dish bursting with health! The brassica (cabbage) family contains valuable phytochemicals that help protect us against cancer. The oils in walnuts are rich in essential omega-3 fatty acids. The sweet, smooth taste of balsamic vinegar comes from being aged in wooden casks for up to 10 years.

1/4	head red cabbage, thinly sliced (4 cups/1 L)	1/4
2 tbsp	water	30 mL
1/2 cup	chopped walnuts	125 mL
2 tbsp	balsamic vinegar	30 mL
1-2 tsp	extra-virgin olive oil (optional)	5-10 mL
1/2 tsp	tamari or soy sauce	2 mL

In covered pan over medium heat, cook cabbage and water for 4 to 5 minutes or until cabbage is wilted. Stir in walnuts, vinegar, oil (if using) and tamari; cook for 2 to 3 minutes.

Makes 4 servings

PER SERVING

calories 117
protein 3 g
fat 9 g
carbohydrate 7 g
dietary fiber 3 g
sodium 43 mg

Excellent source of:
vitamins C and E,
omega-3 fatty acids
Good source of:
magnesium
Source of:
calcium, iron, zinc,
folate, thiamin

% Calories from:
protein 10%
fat 67%
carbohydrate 23%

ROASTED ROOT VEGETABLES

Root vegetables are a part of the autumn harvest that provides a great deal of nourishment and warmth. We have chosen a combination particularly rich in vitamin A; however, you may want to include other vegetables such as parsnips, turnips and squash.

Per serving

calories 267
protein 5 g
fat 6 g
carbohydrate 52 g
dietary fiber 7 g
sodium 199 mg

Excellent source of:
vitamins A and C
Good source of:
magnesium, folate,
thiamin
Source of:
calcium, iron, zinc,
niacin, riboflavin

% Calories from:
protein 7%
fat 18%
carbohydrate 75%

2	carrots	2
2	yams	2
2	potatoes	2
1	large onion	1
2 tbsp	extra-virgin olive oil	30 mL
1 tbsp	chopped fresh herbs (basil, thyme, oregano, dill)	15 mL
1/4 tsp	salt	1 mL
Pinch	pepper	Pinch

Cut vegetables into 2-inch (5 cm) pieces and place in large bowl. Sprinkle with oil, herbs, salt and pepper, tossing well to coat vegetables. Transfer to 13- x 9-inch (3 L) baking dish. Place in 375°F (190°C) oven and bake, uncovered, for 35 to 40 minutes or until vegetables are tender.

Makes 4 servings

SPAGHETTI SQUASH

Spaghetti squash is a marrow that resembles spaghetti when it is cooked and scooped out of the skin with a fork. Many people do not know how to use it, so here is a simple recipe that combines fresh tomatoes and basil as part of a simple summer meal.

I	spaghetti squash	I
1/4 cup	chopped fresh or canned tomatoes	60 mL
1/2 tsp	extra-virgin olive oil (optional)	2 mL
I tsp	chopped fresh basil	5 mL
	Salt and pepper	

PER SERVING

calories 27
protein I g
fat 0.3 g
carbohydrate 6 g
dietary fiber I g
sodium 16 mg

With oil:
calories 32
fat I g

Source of:
magnesium

% Calories from:
protein 10%
fat 8%
carbohydrate 82%

With oil:
% Calories from:
protein 8%
fat 22%
carbohydrate 70%

Cut squash in half lengthwise. Scoop out seeds. Lay cut side of squash down on baking sheet. Add 1/2 cup (125 mL) water to baking sheet and bake in 375°F (190°C) oven for 30 minutes or until indentation remains in skin of squash when pressed. Remove from oven and turn squash over to let steam escape and prevent steam from overcooking squash. Once squash is cool enough to handle, scoop out pulp into bowl using fork or spoon. Stir in tomatoes, olive oil (if using), basil, salt and pepper (if using). Transfer to pan, cover, and heat over medium heat for 3–5 minutes.

Makes 4 servings

Spinach with Garam Masala

Garam masala means warm mixture in Hindi. It is composed of cinnamon, clove, nutmeg, cardamom, mace and black pepper – a combination of spices that have a warming effect on the body. In this modification of a favorite Indian dish, small white cubes of tofu rest on a sea of delicately seasoned, puréed green spinach.

Per serving

calories 51
protein 5 g
fat 4 g
carbohydrate 5 g
dietary fiber 3 g
sodium 202 mg

Excellent source of:
folate, vitamins A
and C
Good source of:
magnesium, riboflavin
Source of:
thiamin, omega-3
fatty acids

% Calories from:
protein 26%
fat 46%
carbohydrate 28%

2	bunches fresh spinach (6 cups/1.5 L)	2
1	small onion, diced	1
2 tsp	canola oil	10 mL
3/4 tsp	garam masala	4 mL
1/2 tsp	ground coriander	2 mL
1/4 tsp	each garlic powder and salt	1 mL
1/2 tsp	lemon juice	2 mL
1/4 cup	finely diced firm tofu	60 mL

Wash spinach well. Steam over medium-high heat for about 3 minutes or just until wilted.

Meanwhile, sauté onion over medium heat in oil for 3 to 5 minutes or until soft. Stir in garam masala, coriander, garlic powder and salt; sauté for 2 to 3 minutes, stirring frequently to prevent spices from sticking.

In bowl of food processor, purée cooked spinach, onion mixture and lemon juice until smooth. Transfer to oven-proof dish and heat in 325°F (160°C) oven for 10 minutes or until tofu is warmed through.

Makes 4 servings

VARIATION:

You can substitute 6 cups (1.5 L) kale for spinach. Add 3 tbsp (45 mL) kale cooking liquid to food processor. The product will have a more fibrous texture than spinach and the added benefit of 550 mg calcium per cup! *(Makes 1 cup/250 mL)*

SPINACH WITH GOMASIO

The next time you go to a Japanese restaurant, order spinach gomae along with vegetarian sushi and perhaps a tofu dish. In the meantime here is our version of this delicious warm spinach salad that you can make at home.

2	bunches packed torn spinach (6 cups/1.5 L)	2
2 tsp	flaxseed or canola oil	10 mL
2 tsp	lemon juice	10 mL
1 tsp	tamari	5 mL
1 tsp	Gomasio (page 59)	5 mL

Wash spinach well and remove stems. Steam spinach in steamer over medium-high heat for 3 minutes or until leaves are just wilted.

Mix oil, lemon juice and tamari in bowl. Stir in steamed spinach and toss. Sprinkle with Gomasio.

Makes 4 servings

PER SERVING

calories 48
protein 3 g
fat 3 g
carbohydrate 4 g
dietary fiber 2 g
sodium 141 mg

Excellent source of:
folate, vitamin A,
omega-3 fatty acids
Source of:
riboflavin, thiamin

% Calories from:
protein 22%
fat 49%
carbohydrate 29%

ZUCCHINI, ONIONS AND TOMATO

Here's another simple vegetable recipe that can be made in minutes during the summer months when zucchini is so abundant in your garden or inexpensive at the farmer's market or supermarket. It provides a good example of the oil-free style of cooking that is found throughout the book. For a fuller description of the cooking method see page 24.

2 cups	chopped fresh or canned tomatoes	500 mL
1	onion, chopped	1
1 tsp	garlic	5 mL
2 cups	chopped or diced zucchini	500 mL
1 tbsp	chopped fresh basil (or 1 tsp/5 mL dried)	15 mL
1/4 tsp	salt	1 mL

In pan, sauté onion and garlic in 3 tbsp (45 mL) of liquid from tomatoes over medium heat for 3 to 5 minutes. Stir in tomatoes, zucchini, basil and salt; cook for 5 minutes. Adjust seasoning.

Makes 4 servings

SAUCES

BLUEBERRY ORANGE SAUCE

This easy-to-make sauce is a treat on pancakes, Vegan Dass Ice Cream (page 192) or Lem-Un-Cheesecake (page 187–88).

2 cups	blueberries, fresh or frozen (thawed)	500 mL
1 cup	apple juice	250 mL
1/4 cup	maple syrup, honey or Sucanat	60 mL
1/2 tsp	cinnamon	2 mL
3/4 cup	orange juice concentrate	175 mL
2–3 tbsp	cornstarch or arrowroot	30-45 mL

Per 1/4-CUP
(60 mL) SERVING

calories 127
protein 1 g
fat 0.3 g
carbohydrate 32 g
dietary fiber 2 g
sodium 6 mg

Excellent source of:
vitamin C
Good source of:
folate
Source of:
magnesium, zinc,
thiamin, vitamin E

% Calories from:
protein 3%
fat 2%
carbohydrate 95%

Heat blueberries, apple juice, maple syrup and cinnamon in saucepan over medium heat until berries are cooked into mash, about 10 minutes.

Combine orange juice concentrate and cornstarch in measuring cup. Stir cornstarch mixture into berry mixture. Bring to boil, simmer 2 to 3 minutes until thickened and serve.

Makes 1-3/4 cups (425 mL)

CRANBERRY GINGER RELISH

Cranberry relish can evoke wonderful memories of Thanksgiving and Christmas. Serve it as a side dish with Stuffed Winter Squash (page 127–28) and Light Mushroom Gravy or Rosemary Gravy (pages 162 and 163).

1/2 cup	red currant jelly or apple jelly	125 mL
1/4 cup	finely diced red onion	60 mL
1	bag (12 oz/340 g) fresh cranberries	1
2 tbsp	orange juice concentrate	30 mL
1/2 tsp	ground ginger	2 mL
1/4 tsp	ground cinnamon	1 mL
1/4 tsp	salt	1 mL
2–4 tbsp	Sucanat or brown sugar	30–60 mL

PER 1/4-CUP
(60 mL) SERVING

calories 79
protein 0.4 g
fat 0.1 g
carbohydrate 20 g
dietary fiber 2 g
sodium 74 mg

% Calories from:
protein 2%
fat 1%
carbohydrate 97%

Heat jelly and onion in pan over medium heat until jelly melts, about 5 minutes. Place cranberries in bowl of food processor and, using pulse action, chop berries but don't purée them. Scrape down sides and pulse for 2 seconds more. Add berries to jelly along with orange juice concentrate, ginger, cinnamon and salt. Reduce heat and simmer, uncovered, for just 10 minutes. Stir occasionally.

Stir in Sucanat.

Makes 2 cups (500 mL)

LIGHT MUSHROOM GRAVY

This recipe is ideal for Stuffed Winter Squash (page 127–28), but it can also be served with mashed potatoes or with veggie burgers. The no-added-oil approach allows you to use as much gravy as you want – in good health! If you use stock cubes or powder, experiment with different brands, as finding flavorful stock cubes makes a big difference. Stocks vary in saltiness, so adjust the amount of tamari accordingly.

3 cups	vegetable stock	750 mL
1 cup	thinly sliced mushrooms	250 mL
1/2 cup	diced onion	125 mL
1/4 cup	each diced carrot and celery	60 mL
2	cloves garlic, chopped	2
3 tbsp	tamari	45 mL
2 tbsp	parsley, chopped	30 mL
1 tbsp	nutritional yeast	15 mL
1/4 tsp	each dried thyme and sage	1 mL
1/2 cup	flour	125 mL
1/4 cup	water	60 mL
	Salt and pepper	

Sauté mushrooms, onion, carrot, celery and garlic in 2 tbsp (30 mL) of the stock, adding more stock if necessary, in pan over medium heat for 5 minutes or until onion is soft. Add additional stock if necessary

Stir in remaining stock, tamari, parsley, yeast, thyme and sage.

Measure flour and water into jar, cover with lid and shake until blended. Strain mixture into pan. Bring to boil, reduce heat and simmer, uncovered, for 15 to 20 minutes. Stir frequently.

Adjust seasoning.

Note: If gravy is too thick, add more stock. If gravy is too thin, simmer, uncovered, to let moisture evaporate.

Makes 4 cups (1 L)

ROSEMARY GRAVY

Can gravy taste good when made without the drippings? Yes! You'll find that the familiar Thanksgiving seasonings of rosemary, thyme and sage make this gravy just as much a part of festive seasons as any gravy you've had before. Double the recipe for leftovers.

1/2 cup	canola oil	125 mL
1/4 cup	each diced onion, carrot and celery	60 mL
2	cloves garlic, chopped	2
1/2 cup	unbleached white flour	125 mL
3 cups	vegetable stock	750 mL
3 tbsp	tamari	45 mL
2 tbsp	chopped fresh parsley	30 mL
2 tsp	dried rosemary	10 mL
1 tsp	dried thyme	5 mL
1/2 tsp	dried sage	2 mL
1/4 tsp	pepper	1 mL
	Salt	

PER 1/4-CUP
(60 mL) SERVING

calories 210
protein 3 g
fat 18 g
carbohydrate 10 g
dietary fiber 2 g
sodium 420 mg

Good source of:
vitamin A
Source of:
iron, folate, thiamin

% Calories from:
protein 5%
fat 76%
carbohydrate 19%

Sauté onion, carrot, celery and garlic in canola oil in pan over medium heat for 5 minutes. Stir in flour to absorb the oil and cook for another 5 minutes, stirring frequently. Remove pot from heat for 3 minutes to cool. (If you add stock to hot mix, flour will lump.) Return to heat and slowly pour in stock, stirring constantly.

Add tamari, parsley, rosemary, thyme, sage and pepper. Bring to boil, reduce heat and simmer, uncovered, for 15 to 20 minutes. Stir frequently. Adjust seasoning.

Note: If gravy is too thick, add more stock. If gravy is too thin, simmer, uncovered, to let moisture evaporate.

Makes 1-1/2 cups (375 mL)

PEANUT SAUCE

This can be used as a dipping sauce for Fresh Vegetable Salad Roll (page 70) or for bread. Use it as a sauce with vegetables, served over noodles. This sauce keeps well in the refrigerator for up to 2 weeks; however, it will thicken as it sits. When you'd like to use it, thin with warm water to desired consistency.

PER 2 TBSP
(30 mL)

calories 104
protein 4 g
fat 8 g
carbohydrate 5 g
dietary fiber 1 g
sodium 149 mg

Source of:
iron, magnesium, zinc,
folate, niacin, thiamin

% Calories from:
protein 15%
fat 65%
carbohydrate 20%

1/2 cup	unsweetened peanut butter	125 mL
1/2 cup	warm water or rice milk	125 mL
2–3 tbsp	lemon juice	30–45 mL
1 tbsp	miso	15 mL
1 tbsp	finely chopped green onion	15 mL
2 tsp	Sucanat or brown sugar	10 mL
2 tsp	tamari or soy sauce	10 mL
1/4 tsp	each garlic powder and ground ginger	1 mL
Pinch	cayenne (optional)	Pinch

Blend peanut butter and warm water into smooth paste in bowl using whisk.

Stir in lemon juice, miso, green onion, Sucanat, tamari, garlic, ginger and cayenne (if using), mixing until smooth.

Makes 1 cup (250 mL)

TAMARIND DATE SAUCE

Tamarind is an Indian fruit that grows in a pod. This sauce, made from a concentrate of the fruit, adds unique lemony sharpness when served as a condiment with Potato Subji (page 151), with curries or in an Indonesian Roll-up (page 114). Tamarind paste can be purchased at East Indian groceries. While you're there, enjoy the aromas of exotic ingredients and stock up on papadums, almonds and spices such as curry powder and paste, garam masala and cumin.

3/4 cup	water	175 mL
3/4 cup	pitted chopped dates	175 mL
3 tbsp	tamarind paste	45 mL
2 tbsp	apple cider vinegar	30 mL
1 tbsp	peeled grated gingerroot	15 mL
2 tsp	orange juice concentrate	10 mL
1/2 tsp	garam masala	2 mL
Pinch	salt	Pinch

Per 1 tbsp (15 mL)

calories 21
protein 0.2 g
fat trace
carbohydrate 6 g
dietary fiber 1 g
sodium 9 mg

% Calories from:
protein 3%
fat 2%
carbohydrate 95%

Pour water over dates and let sit for 30 minutes. Place dates with soaking water, tamarind paste, vinegar, ginger, orange juice concentrate, garam masala and salt in bowl of food processor and blend until smooth, occasionally scraping down sides of bowl. (This sauce can be kept refrigerated for several weeks.)

Makes 1-1/4 cups (300 mL)

TERIYAKI SAUCE

Teriyaki sauce is common to Japanese cuisine. It adds both sweet and salty flavors to the food with which it is blended. The first choice for this recipe is sake, a Japanese rice wine that has a clean but distinctive taste and adds a lot of character. If you prefer not to use alcohol in your cooking, the sake can be replaced with stock, preferably a no-salt version. Teriyaki sauce can be added to stir-fries, tofu or rice.

PER 1 TBSP (15 mL)

calories 14
protein 0.4 g
fat trace
carbohydrate 3 g
dietary fiber 0.1 g
sodium 128 mg

% Calories from:
protein 12%
fat 0%
carbohydrate 88%

1/2 cup	light or regular tamari	125 mL
1/2 cup	sake or vegetable stock	125 mL
1/2 cup	mirin	125 mL
1/2 cup	packed brown sugar	125 mL
1/2	onion, chopped	1/2
3 tbsp	thinly sliced gingerroot (unpeeled)	45 mL
4	cloves garlic, chopped	4
1 tbsp	cornstarch	15 mL
1 tbsp	water	15 mL

Bring tamari, sake, mirin, brown sugar, onion, ginger and garlic to boil in pan over high heat. Immediately reduce heat and simmer for 10 minutes

Dissolve cornstarch in water and stir into pan. Cook, stirring, until thickened. After sauce thickens, simmer for 3 minutes, then strain. The sauce keeps in the refrigerator for several weeks.

Makes 2 cups (500 mL)

TOMATO-MISO SAUCE

Miso gives this sauce robust flavor. If you're serving this sauce with noodles, you'll need 2 to 3 ounces (60 to 90 grams) of noodles per person. An easy way to gauge this is to grasp in your hand, for each adult, a bunch of dry noodles the size of a quarter (or the diameter of a loonie for a very hungry adult).

2 tbsp	water or 1 tbsp (15 mL) extra-virgin olive oil	30 mL
1/2	onion, diced	1/2
1/2 cup	each diced carrot and celery	125 mL
1/4 cup	diced sweet red pepper	60 mL
2	cloves garlic, chopped	2
3 cups	diced fresh or canned tomatoes (28 oz/796 mL), diced	750 mL
1	can (5 oz/150 g) tomato paste	1
1 tsp	dried basil	5 mL
1/2 tsp	dried oregano	2 mL
1/8 tsp	black pepper	0.5 mL
2 tbsp	miso	30 mL
2 tbsp	water	30 mL
2 tbsp	Sucanat or brown sugar	30 mL
1/4 tsp	salt (optional)	1 mL

In pan over medium heat, sauté onion, carrot, celery, red pepper and garlic in 2 tbsp (30 mL) water, adding more water if necessary, or 1 tbsp (15 mL) oil for 5 minutes.

Stir in tomatoes, paste, basil, oregano, and pepper; cover, reduce heat and simmer for 20 minutes. Mix together miso and water to form a paste; stir into sauce along with Sucanat. Heat through and adjust seasoning.

Makes about five 1-cup (250 mL) servings

PER SERVING

calories 123
protein 5 g
fat 1 g
carbohydrate 27 g
dietary fiber 4 g
sodium 523 mg

With oil:
calories 147
fat 4 g

Excellent source of:
vitamins A and C
Good source of:
iron, magnesium
Source of:
folate, calcium, zinc, niacin, riboflavin, thiamin

% Calories from:
protein 13%
fat 10%
carbohydrate 77%

With oil:
% Calories from:
protein 11%
fat 25%
carbohydrate 64%

TOMATO SAUCES

If you're cooking for one or two people, here are three easy ways to add protein and iron to a cup of your favorite commercial tomato sauce (or to the recipe on page 168–69). Serve these sauces with noodles, veggie burgers, or in any other way that you normally use tomato sauce. Double or triple recipes to give the desired amount of sauce.

TOMATO SAUCE WITH ADUKI BEANS

In Japan, *aduki* (also called adzuki) beans have a reputation as an excellent source of dietary iron. In fact, when a Japanese girl has her first menstrual period, the family will often honor the occasion by serving a dish of red beans and rice called Sekihan, which replenishes her iron! The small red beans can be cooked in 45 minutes after soaking, or in 90 minutes without soaking (see legumes chart in appendix, page 200). Cooked beans freeze well, so keep a few portions in the freezer in plastic containers for instant use.

1 cup	tomato sauce	250 mL
3/4 cup	cooked or canned aduki beans, mashed	175 mL

Heat tomato sauce and beans.

Makes 1-3/4 cups (425 mL)

Tomato Sauce with Textured Soy Protein (Happy Camper's Tomato Sauce)

Textured soy protein, also known as textured vegetable protein or TVP, is a simple way to add protein and minerals to tomato sauce, soups and casseroles without added fat. Since it is dehydrated, it is extremely light and has a long shelf life, so it's handy for back-packing and camping trips.

1 cup	tomato sauce	250 mL
2 tbsp	textured soy protein	30 mL

Heat tomato sauce, add textured soy protein and simmer 15 minutes.

Makes 1-1/8 cups (275 mL)

Tomato Sauce with Tofu

Here is yet another use for this very versatile product – tofu can be mashed into tomato sauce and used with all sorts of pasta dishes. Instead, you may prefer to purée the mixture in a blender, giving a smooth creamy texture; no one will know the dish contains tofu unless you tell them. You'll be adding iron, protein and zinc (and calcium when using tofu made with calcium).

1 cup	tomato sauce	250 mL
1/2 cup	medium-firm tofu	125 mL

Mash tofu and add tomato sauce or combine in a blender; heat in saucepan.

Makes 1-1/2 cups (375 mL)

Per recipe with textured soy protein:
calories 102
protein 8 g
fat 1 g
iron 3 mg
zinc 1 mg

% Calories from:
protein 15%
fat 4%
carbohydrate 81%

Per recipe with tofu:
calories 176
protein 14 g
fat 7 g
iron 4 mg
zinc 3 mg

% Calories from:
protein 30%
fat 31%
carbohydrate 39%

DESSERTS

Apple Kanten

A traditional Japanese fruit dessert, *kanten* is a very simple dish that is easy to prepare. Serve it after a heavier meal or on a hot summer evening.

4 cups	apple juice	1 L
1/8 tsp	each ground cinnamon and nutmeg	0.5 mL
Pinch	each ground allspice, cloves and salt	Pinch
1/3 cup	agar flakes	75 mL
1 cup	firm fruit such as blueberries, diced cantaloupe or sliced banana	250 mL

Place 1 cup (250 mL) of the apple juice in small jar along with cinnamon, nutmeg, allspice, cloves and salt; cover and shake vigorously until blended. Pour into pot along with remaining juice. Bring to boil over medium heat. Immediately reduce heat to low, stir in agar and cook, stirring occasionally, for 5 minutes or until agar dissolves. Pour into serving bowl and refrigerate for 4 to 5 hours or until set. Just before serving, stir with whisk and stir in fruit.

VARIATION:

For a pretty red kanten, use sweetened cranberry juice or a cranberry-apple blend in place of apple juice.

Makes 4 servings

Agar

Agar, also known as agar agar, is a seaweed derivative that is processed into near-transparent powder, flakes or bars. The wonderful feature of agar is that it gels, thereby making it an excellent vegetarian replacement for gelatin. Since the densities of the powder, flakes and bar differ, take care to use the specific product called for in a recipe. Agar needs to be thoroughly dissolved in liquid before it will gel. A standard rule of thumb for thickening fruit juice is 1 tbsp (15 mL) agar flakes to 1 cup (250 mL) of juice.

APPLE PEAR CRUMBLE

Many other fruits can be substituted for apples and pears in this recipe. Try peaches or nectarines with blueberries, raspberries or blackberries, and use a total of 7 to 8 cups of fruit.

PER SERVING

calories 309
protein 4 g
fat 5 g
carbohydrate 64 g
dietary fiber 4 g
sodium 5 mg

Excellent source of:
iron, riboflavin,
thiamin
Good source of:
calcium, folate,
omega-3 fatty acids
Source of:
magnesium, zinc

% *Calories from:*
protein 6%
fat 15%
carbohydrate 79%

3	unpeeled apples, cored and chopped	3
3	unpeeled pears, cored and chopped	3
2 tbsp	lemon juice	30 mL
3 tbsp	maple syrup	45 mL
1/4 cup	raisins	60 mL

TOPPING:

2 cups	rolled oats	500 mL
1/4 cup	chopped walnuts	60 mL
1/2 cup	orange juice concentrate	125 mL
1/3 cup	water	75 mL
3 tbsp	maple syrup	45 mL
1 1/2 tsp	whole wheat flour	7 mL
1/2 tsp	ground cinnamon	2 mL
1/8 tsp	nutmeg	0.5 mL

Toss lemon juice with fruit in 8-inch (2 L) baking dish. Drizzle maple syrup and sprinkle raisins over top.

TOPPING:

In bowl combine oats, walnuts, orange juice concentrate, water, maple syrup, flour, cinnamon and nutmeg. Let mixture sit for 10 minutes for oats to absorb liquid. Spread mixture evenly over fruit and bake in 350°F (180°C) oven for 25 to 30 minutes or until golden brown.

Makes 6 servings

APPLE SPICE CAKE

This lovely cake can be used as a family dessert or for a festive occasion like a wedding or birthday. Serve it plain or with your favorite icing.

3 cups	whole wheat pastry flour	750 mL
1 tbsp	baking powder	15 mL
2 tsp	ground cinnamon	10 mL
1 tsp	baking soda	5 mL
1 tsp	each ground cloves, allspice, nutmeg and ginger	5 mL
1/2 tsp	salt	2 mL
1 cup	maple syrup, corn syrup or honey	250 mL
1 cup	soy or dairy milk	250 mL
2/3 cup	canola oil	150 mL
2 tbsp	ground flaxseed or 2 eggs (see page 189)	30 mL
2 cups	grated apples	500 mL
1 cup	raisins	250 mL
1 cup	chopped walnuts or pecans	250 mL

PER PIECE

calories 208
protein 3 g
fat 10 g
carbohydrate 29 g
dietary fiber 3 g
sodium 147 mg

Good source of:
magnesium
Source of:
calcium, iron, zinc,
thiamin, vitamin E

% Calories from:
protein 6%
fat 41%
carbohydrate 53%

In bowl, mix flour, baking powder, cinnamon, baking soda, cloves, allspice, nutmeg, ginger and salt. In large bowl, combine maple syrup, milk, oil and flaxseed. Stir flour mixture into wet ingredients until blended. Fold in apples, raisins and nuts. Do not overmix. Pour into oiled and floured 13- x 9-inch (3 L) baking pan. Bake in 350°F (180°C) oven for 35 to 40 minutes or until a toothpick inserted into cake comes out clean.

Makes 24 pieces

Baked Stuffed Apples

This recipe is equally tasty made with McIntosh apples, which are quick to cook, or other varieties such as Golden Delicious or Granny Smith, which may take longer.

4	baking apples	4
1/4 cup	tahini	60 mL
1/4 cup	raisins	60 mL
2 tsp	lemon juice	10 mL
1/2 tsp	grated lemon rind	2 mL
2 tsp	maple syrup or Sucanat	10 mL
1/4 tsp	cinnamon	1 mL
Pinch	ground cardamom (optional)	Pinch
1/2 cup	orange juice	125 mL

Pierce top of apples holding paring knife at a 45° angle to stems. Rotate knife around top to produce small cone-shaped tops. Set tops aside. Using melon baller or teaspoon, remove core from apples, being careful not to pierce the bottom of apples.

In small bowl, stir together tahini, raisins, lemon juice, rind, maple syrup, cinnamon and cardamom (if using).

Fill apple cavities almost to top with raisin mixture. Replace apple tops. Set apples in baking dish, pour orange juice over and bake in a 300°F (150°C) oven for 15 minutes or until soft when pierced with toothpick.

Variation:
Replace tahini with 3 figs that have been soaked overnight, stems removed, and chopped.

Makes 4 servings

Blueberry Corn Muffins

The combination of blueberries and cornmeal makes a delicious muffin with a mild sweetness. Serve these muffins warm for breakfast or as a superb accompaniment to a hearty soup.

2 cups	whole wheat pastry flour	500 mL
1-1/2 tsp	baking powder	7 mL
1/2 tsp	baking soda	2 mL
1/2 tsp	salt	2 mL
1 cup	cornmeal	250 mL
1-1/2 cups	soy or dairy milk	375 mL
1/3 cup	canola oil	75 mL
1/3 cup	maple syrup, honey or corn syrup	75 mL
1 tbsp	ground flaxseed or 1 egg (see page 189)	15 mL
1-1/2 cups	blueberries, fresh or frozen (thawed)	375 mL

PER MUFFIN

calories 204
protein 5 g
fat 7 g
carbohydrate 32 g
dietary fiber 4 g
sodium 197 mg

Good source of:
magnesium
Source of:
calcium, iron, zinc,
folate, riboflavin,
thiamin, vitamin E

% Calories from:
protein 9%
fat 32%
carbohydrate 59%

Mix flour, baking powder, baking soda and salt in bowl.

In large bowl, combine cornmeal, milk, oil, maple syrup and flaxseed and let sit for 3 minutes.

Stir flour into milk mixture just until blended. Do not overmix.

Fold in blueberries, spoon into lightly oiled muffin tins and bake in 400°F (200°C) oven for about 20 minutes or until golden brown.

Makes 12 muffins

BLUEBERRY MINCE TARTS

Blueberries and cranberries, two of Canada's most delicious fruit crops, are combined in this mouth-watering tart filling, created by dietitian Jean Fremont and recipe developer Georgina Seifert of Delta Nutrition Systems. With all the heavy foods around during the holiday season, these tarts are refreshingly light.

PER TART, WITH PASTRY

calories 217
protein 3 g
fat 6 g
carbohydrate 40 g
dietary fiber 3 g
sodium 171 mg

Source of:
calcium, iron, magnesium, niacin, riboflavin, thiamin

% Calories from:
protein 5%
fat 24%
carbohydrate 71%

BLUEBERRY FILLING:

1-1/4 cups	sultana raisins	300 mL
1-1/4 cups	golden raisins	300 mL
1/2 cup	dried cranberries	125 mL
1/2 cup	Sucanat or brown sugar	125 mL
1/3 cup	candied mixed peel	75 mL
2 tbsp	fruit juice or brandy	30 mL
1 tbsp	lemon juice	15 mL
1 tsp	grated lemon rind	5 mL
1 tsp	ground cinnamon	5 mL
1/2 tsp	each ground cloves, ginger and nutmeg	2 mL
4 cups	blueberries, fresh or frozen	1 L

Combine raisins, cranberries, sugar, mixed peel, fruit juice, lemon juice and rind, cinnamon, cloves, ginger and nutmeg in large bowl. Stir in blueberries.

WHOLE WHEAT PASTRY:

Rolling pastry is easy – no flour on the countertop to clean up afterward – if you roll it between 2 clean plastic bags (cut down 2 sides and opened).

1-1/2 cups	whole wheat pastry flour	375 mL
1-1/2 cups	unbleached or all-purpose flour	375 mL
1 tbsp	baking powder	15 mL
1/2 tsp	salt	2 mL
1/2 cup	safflower, sunflower or corn oil	125 mL
1/2 cup	ice water	125 mL

Let several ice cubes stand in glass of water to make ice water. Meanwhile, in bowl, stir flours, baking powder and salt with whisk or fork until well mixed. Stir in oil, tossing mixture with fork until small balls form. Sprinkle ice water gradually into mixture, tossing with fork until all flour is incorporated. Gather into 2 balls.

Roll out each ball between plastic bags or sheets of waxed paper. To cut out tarts, use 4-inch (10 cm) jar lid. Lift dough circles with egg lifter and place in lightly oiled or nonstick muffin tin.

Place slightly more than 1/4 cup (60 mL) blueberry filling into each tart shell. Bake in 400°F (200°C) oven for 17 to 20 minutes or until crust begins to brown. Cool before removing tarts from cups.

Makes 20 tarts

BROWN RICE PUDDING

Brown rice quickly becomes a mainstay and a favorite in a vegetarian's kitchen pantry. It provides a wider assortment of trace minerals and B vitamins than its refined counterpart, white rice. Cook it in large batches and incorporate leftovers in this comforting desserts or in International Roll-ups (page 114–15). This pudding also makes a fine breakfast food.

PER SERVING

calories 302
protein 7 g
fat 3 g
carbohydrate 63 g
dietary fiber 3 g
sodium 11 mg

Excellent source of:
magnesium, thiamin
Good source of: iron,
zinc
Source of:
niacin, riboflavin

% Calories from:
protein 9%
fat 10%
carbohydrate 81%

2 cups	soy or dairy milk	500 mL
4 cups	cooked brown rice	1 L
1/2 cup	raisins or chopped dates	125 mL
1/4 cup	maple syrup	60 mL
1/2 tsp	grated lemon rind	2 mL
2 tsp	lemon juice	10 mL
1 tsp	vanilla extract	5 mL
1/2 tsp	ground cinnamon	2 mL
1/8 tsp	each ground cloves and nutmeg	0.5 mL

Pour milk over rice in bowl. Stir in raisins, maple syrup, lemon rind and juice, vanilla, cinnamon, cloves and nutmeg, mixing well. Pour into 8-inch (2 L) square baking dish. Cover and bake in 325°F (160°C) oven for 30 to 40 minutes or until set.

Makes 5 servings

CASHEW BALLS

These energy-packed balls are ideal for hiking trips, when space is at a premium. Eat one at the top of the mountain, and you'll have a peak experience!

1 cup	cashew butter	250 mL
1/3 cup	chopped, roasted, unsalted cashews	75 mL
1/4 cup	currants	60 mL
2 tbsp	tofu milk powder or powdered milk	30 mL
1 tbsp	maple syrup or honey	15 mL
1/4 tsp	grated lemon rind	1 mL
2 tsp	lemon juice	10 mL
1/2 tsp	vanilla extract	2 mL
1/4 tsp	ground cinnamon	1 mL
1/4 tsp	ground cardamom	1 mL
2 tbsp	finely shredded coconut	30 mL

PER BALL

calories 207
protein 6 g
fat 15 g
carbohydrate 13 g
dietary fiber 1 g
sodium 187 mg

Good source of:
magnesium
Source of:
iron, zinc, folate,
thiamin, vitamin E

% Calories from:
protein 10%
fat 64%
carbohydrate 26%

Combine cashew butter, cashews, currants, tofu milk powder, maple syrup, lemon rind, juice, vanilla, cinnamon and cardamom together in bowl.

Roll 1 tbsp (15 mL) of mixture between palms into a golf ball size. Roll ball in coconut to coat.

Makes 10 balls

Tofu milk powder, available at local health food stores, is a handy item to keep in your kitchen cupboard. It's easily mixed and can be used wherever soy or cow's milks are called for.

Chocolate Cream Couscous Cake

Executive chef Ron Pickarski is a five-time medal winner at the International Culinary Olympics in Germany for his plant-based vegetarian displays. From his *Friendly Foods* cookbook (published by Ten Speed Press), here's a simply delicious no-bake cake,* representative of Pickarski's genius with foods. This recipe also works well if you decrease the amount of Sucanat in the cake to 3/4 cup (175 mL).

PER SERVING

calories 244
protein 5 g
fat 10 g
carbohydrate 37 g
dietary fiber 2 g
sodium 43 mg

Good source of:
magnesium
Source of:
iron, zinc, riboflavin, thiamin

% Calories from:
protein 8%
fat 35%
carbohydrate 57%

3/4 cup	pecans	175 mL
2-1/2 cups	water	625 mL
1-1/2 cups	Sucanat	375 mL
1/4 cup	cocoa powder	60 mL
1 cup	raw couscous	250 mL
1 tbsp	vanilla extract	15 mL

Roast pecans in 300°F (150°C) oven for about 30 minutes (or a little less time; take care not to burn them). Remove from oven and let cool. Grind in food processor for 5 to 10 seconds until consistency of coarse meal. Set aside.

In saucepan, stir together water, Sucanat, cocoa and couscous. Bring to simmer and cook until thickened, 5 to 10 minutes. Add vanilla and stir well. Spread mixture in 9-inch (2.5 L) springform pan. Sprinkle 1/4 cup (60 mL) of the pecan meal over the couscous cake.

FILLING:

10 oz	chocolate chips, barley malt or regular	286 g
2	pkg (each 10 oz/300 g) firm silken tofu (at room temperature)	2
3 tbsp	maple syrup	45 mL

Melt chocolate chips in small saucepan over low heat, stirring constantly. Transfer to blender, add tofu and maple syrup and blend until smooth. Pour Filling over cake and top with remaining pecan meal. Refrigerate until set, about 2 hours. Serve cold.

Makes 16 servings

*Used with permission.

CRANBERRY PECAN MUFFINS

Maple syrup offsets the tartness of cranberries in these outstanding muffins, an inspired creation of Brenda Davis, co-author of *Becoming Vegetarian*. Stock your freezer with fresh cranberries when they are in season as you'll want to make these muffins often.

2-1/2 cups	cranberries, fresh or frozen (thawed)	625 mL
1/2 cup	maple syrup	125 mL
1 tsp	grated orange or lemon rind	5 mL
1/2 cup	Sucanat or packed brown sugar	125 mL
1	pkg (10 oz/300 g) soft tofu	1
1/2 cup	soy or dairy milk	125 mL
1/3 cup	canola oil	75 mL
1 tsp	vanilla extract	5 mL
2 cups	whole wheat flour	500 mL
2 tsp	baking powder	10 mL
2 tsp	cinnamon	10 mL
1 tsp	baking soda	5 mL
1/2 tsp each ground cardamom, allspice, cloves and salt		2 mL
1 cup	coarsely chopped pecans	250 mL

PER MUFFIN

calories 266
protein 5 g
fat 13 g
carbohydrate 35 g
dietary fiber 4 g
sodium 262 mg

Good source of: magnesium, zinc, thiamin
Source of: calcium, iron, folate, riboflavin

% *Calories from:*
protein 8%
fat 43%
carbohydrate 49%

Cook 1-1/2 cups (375 mL) of the cranberries with maple syrup and rind in pan over medium heat until berries have popped and liquid is thick. Chop remaining cranberries in food processor or with a knife. Stir into cooked berries and let cool.

Meanwhile, combine Sucanat, tofu, milk, oil and vanilla in large bowl and beat together well. Mix flour, baking powder, cinnamon, baking soda, cardamom, allspice, cloves and salt in small bowl. Stir cranberries into wet ingredients, mixing well. Stir in dry ingredients along with pecans just until blended. Fill paper muffin cups and bake in 375°F (190°C) oven for 30 minutes or until inserted toothpick comes out clean.

Makes 12 large muffins

FIGGY PUDDING

Figs have been gaining popularity now that we realize that they are sources of calcium. This elegant way of serving figs combines the goodness of apple juice, the smoothness of silken tofu and the sweetness of figs and contains 135 mg of calcium per serving.

10	dried golden figs, stems removed	10
1-1/2 cups	apple juice	375 mL
1	pkg (10 oz/300 g) firm silken tofu	1
1 tbsp	lemon juice	15 mL
2 tsp	Sucanat or brown sugar	10 mL
1/4 tsp	ground cinnamon	1 mL
1/4 tsp	vanilla extract	1 mL
Pinch	ground cloves	Pinch
1 tbsp	slivered almonds (optional)	15 mL

Soak figs in apple juice in refrigerator for 12 hours.

Combine figs, apple juice, tofu, lemon juice, Sucanat, cinnamon, vanilla and cloves in blender and purée for 2 to 3 minutes until very smooth, occasionally scraping down sides of bowl. Scoop into 3 small serving bowls or 3 wide-mouthed champagne glasses. Garnish with almonds (if using).

Makes 3 servings

HOLIDAY PIE TOPPING

This low-fat alternative to whipped cream is a great accompaniment
to Pumpkin Pie (page 190) or Blueberry Mince Tarts (page 178–79)
or apple pie.

1	pkg (10 oz/300 g) firm silken tofu	1
1/4 cup	maple syrup	60 mL
1 tbsp	lemon juice	15 mL
1 tsp	vanilla extract	5 mL

In blender or food processor, purée tofu, maple syrup, lemon juice
and vanilla for about 1 minute or until perfectly smooth. Chill for
1 to 2 hours. Spread over cooled pie or serve on each individual pie
serving.

Makes 4 servings

PER SERVING

calories 100
protein 5 g
fat 2 g
carbohydrate 16 g
dietary fiber 0 g
sodium 28 mg

Source of:
iron, magnesium, zinc,
thiamin

% Calories from:
protein 20%
fat 19%
carbohydrate 61%

Lemon Sesame Cookies

Thanks to Brenda Davis, dietitian and inspired baker, for these exceptionally delectable cookies. They have a moist cakelike texture and lemon-sesame flavor. Serve them with a fresh fruit salad or pack them in your children's lunch, or your own.

Per cookie

calories 82
protein 1 g
fat 4 g
carbohydrate 10 g
dietary fiber 0.5 g
sodium 52 mg

Source of:
iron, thiamin

% Calories from:
protein 7%
fat 45%
carbohydrate 48%

2 cups	unbleached or all-purpose flour	500 mL
1/2 cup	sesame seeds	125 mL
1/4 cup	wheat germ	60 mL
2 tsp	baking powder	10 mL
1/2 tsp	salt	2 mL
1	pkg (10 oz/300 g) soft tofu	1
1/2 cup	maple syrup	125 mL
1/4 cup	sesame oil	60 mL
1/4 cup	canola or sunflower oil	60 mL
1/4 cup	Sucanat or brown sugar	60 mL
1 tsp	vanilla extract	5 mL
1 tsp	lemon extract	5 mL
1 tsp	grated lemon rind	5 mL

Combine flour, sesame seeds, wheat germ, baking powder and salt in bowl.

In another bowl, mash tofu well. Stir in maple syrup, oils, Sucanat, vanilla, lemon extract and lemon rind. Stir flour mixture into wet ingredients, mixing quickly. Drop by teaspoonfuls onto oiled baking sheet. Bake in 350°F (180°C) oven for about 12 minutes or until golden brown, rotating baking sheet after 5 to 7 minutes for even baking. Remove to rack to let cool. Store in covered jar or covered plastic container.

Makes 36 cookies

LEM-UN-CHEESECAKE WITH CRUMB CRUST

This pie can be made quickly from ingredients you keep on hand in your kitchen. You can use a commercial Graham crust or make the flavorful crumb crust given here. Once chilled, decorate the top of the cheesecake with fresh fruit such as strawberries, peaches and kiwifruit or with Blueberry Orange Sauce (page 160).

CRUMB CRUST:

This excellent crust was developed by Victoria Harrison, co-author of *Becoming Vegetarian*. Ground flaxseed offers a nutty flavor and works best with Pumpkin Pie (page 190), whereas gluten flour provides a lighter taste and works best with the Lem-Un-Cheesecake.

1-1/4 cups	Graham crumbs or ground cereal (such as Nature's Path)	300 mL
3/4 cup	quick-cooking oat flakes	175 mL
3 tbsp	ground flaxseed or gluten flour	45 mL
1/3 cup	canola oil	90 mL
1/3 cup	water	90 mL
2 tsp	vanilla extract	10 mL

In bowl, stir together crumbs, oat flakes and flaxseed. In small bowl, whisk together oil, water and vanilla. Using fork, quickly stir oil mixture into crumb mixture.

Using fingers, work oil mixture well into crumbs for a few seconds. Spray 9- or 10-inch (23 or 25 cm) pie plate with vegetable spray or coat lightly with oil. Press crumb mixture firmly and evenly onto sides and bottom of pie plate.

PER SERVING

calories 287
protein 9 g
fat 15g
carbohydrate 31 g
dietary fiber 2 g
sodium 142 mg

Good source of:
iron, magnesium
Source of:
zinc, riboflavin,
thiamin, vitamin E

% Calories from:
protein 12%
fat 46%
carbohydrate 43%

FILLING:

2	pkg (each 10 oz/300 g) firm silken tofu	2
1/3 cup	maple syrup or honey	75 mL
4 tsp	grated lemon rind	20 mL
1/4 cup	lemon juice	60 mL
1 1/2 tsp	vanilla extract	7 mL

In bowl of food processor, purée tofu, maple syrup, lemon rind, lemon juice and vanilla extract, scraping down sides of bowl occasionally. Pour mixture into unbaked pie shell and bake in 350°F (180°C) oven for 1 hour or until toothpick comes out clean and crust is beginning to brown. Chill before serving.

Makes 8 servings

FLAXSEED

Flaxseeds, also known as linseeds, are reddish-brown oval seeds, slightly bigger than sesame seeds. Mucilage gums present in ground flaxseed attract and hold water or other liquids. Due to this quality, a tablespoon of ground flaxseed gives a binding quality similar to that provided by an egg when used in baked goods and is an excellent cholesterol-free egg replacer for use in baked items. It can be purchased ground (Omega Nutrition's Nutri-Flax, see Appendix III) or you can grind whole seeds in your blender. Whole flaxseeds do not require refrigeration, but ground flaxseed should be stored in the freezer to prevent the omega-3 fatty acids from becoming rancid once seeds are crushed.

Ground flaxseed helps to produce a moist, light product and provides essential omega-3 fatty acids.

1 tbsp (15 mL) of ground flaxseed plus 3 tbsp (45 mL) water is equivalent to 1 egg.

Mix ground flaxseed and water in a small bowl and let sit for 1 to 2 minutes. Add to recipe as you would add an egg.

PUMPKIN PIE

This filling is adapted from a recipe developed by Mori-Nu Nutritional Foods, using their creamy smooth silken tofu. It can be baked in the Crumb Crust on page 187. Use the remainder of the package of tofu to make Holiday Pie Topping (page 185) or Fruit Shake (page 36).

PER SERVING

calories 332
protein 8 g
fat 14 g
carbohydrate 43 g
dietary fiber 4 g
sodium 139 mg

Excellent source of:
vitamin A
Good source of:
iron, magnesium, zinc
Source of:
calcium, folate,
riboflavin, thiamin

% Calories from:
protein 10%
fat 29%
carbohydrate 61%

1-1/2	pkg (each 10 oz/300 g) firm silken tofu	1-1/2
1-3/4 cups	pumpkin, canned	425 mL
	(2 cups, 500 mL) cooked	
2/3 cup	maple syrup or honey	150 mL
1 tsp	vanilla extract	5 mL
1 1/2 tsp	ground cinnamon	7 mL
3/4 tsp	ground ginger	4 mL
1/4 tsp	each ground nutmeg and cloves	1 mL
	unbaked Crumb Crust (page 187)	

Blend tofu in a food processor or blender until creamy smooth. Add pumpkin, maple syrup, vanilla, cinnamon, ginger, nutmeg and cloves; blend well. Pour into Crumb Crust and bake in 375°F (190°C) oven for 1 hour or until the middle of the pie is set.

Makes 8 servings

No-Bake Chocolate Chews

These fast and easy chocolate squares are a welcome treat for those with a sweet tooth. You may wish to use carob chips instead of chocolate chips.

1/2 cup	almond or peanut butter	125 mL
1/2 cup	maple syrup, honey or corn syrup	125 mL
1/3 cup	chocolate chips or 2.5 oz (75 g) semisweet baking chocolate	75 mL
1 tsp	vanilla extract	5 mL
2 cups	crispy rice cereal or corn flakes	500 mL
1/2 cup	chopped unsalted almonds or walnuts	125 mL
2 tbsp	wheat germ	30 mL

PER SQUARE OR COOKIE

calories 85
protein 2 g
fat 5 g
carbohydrate 9 g
dietary fiber 1 g
sodium 2 mg

Source of:
magnesium, zinc

% Calories from:
protein 7%
fat 53%
carbohydrate 40%

Heat nut butter and maple syrup in pan over medium-high heat until nut butter softens and mixes easily with syrup. Lower heat to simmer and cook for 2 minutes, stirring constantly. Stir in chocolate chips until melted. Remove from heat and stir in vanilla. Mix in cereal, nuts and wheat germ. Drop from teaspoon onto baking sheet lined with waxed paper or pat into lightly oiled 8-inch (2 L) square cake pan. Refrigerate until firm.

Makes 24

Vegan Dass Ice Cream

If you have a food processor, a Green Power juice extractor or a Champion juicer, you can start making the simplest, lowest fat, nondairy ice cream imaginable. All you do is freeze some bananas overnight on a tray or in a plastic bag and then take a few minutes to process them into a smooth dessert. The nutritional analysis is exceptional, because the only ingredient is bananas! After you try the basic recipe, experiment with some of your own variations such as adding some carob, chocolate powder, blueberries or strawberries.

| 4 | bananas, peeled, broken into quarters and frozen | 4 |

Place bananas in food processor and process until smooth or process through Champion juicer. Serve immediately.

Makes 4 servings

VARIATION:
For a sorbet-type frozen dessert, use berries, mango, pineapple, or kiwi.

PER SERVING

calories 105
protein 1 g
fat 1 g
carbohydrate 27 g
dietary fiber 2 g
sodium 1 mg

Source of:
magnesium, folate, riboflavin

% Calories from:
protein 4%
fat 4%
carbohydrate 92%

CEREAL GRAINS – THE STAFF OF LIFE

The use of cereal grains can be traced back to the dawn of civilization. From earliest times, tribes focused their attention on primitive agricultural techniques that centered around growing cereal grasses. As populations grew and developed their identity, particular grains became associated with specific regions. Many nations of the world have a cereal that can be traced to their origins. The Russians have buckwheat, the Chinese and Japanese have rice, the Scottish and Irish have oats, central America has corn and the great plains of Canada and the United States have wheat and rye.

Grains, the small fruit or kernel of cereal grasses, are the edible seeds of those grasses. What has made them so important in the history of the world is their nutritional composition. Grains are made up of four distinct parts with protein distributed throughout all four. The first layer is the husk, also known as the chaff. The chaff is the tough protective layer that surrounds the seed and keeps it protected from the natural elements during its growth. The husk is indigestible for humans and once removed, it is discarded.

The next part is the bran. This layer surrounds the seed and is rich in vitamins, minerals and fiber, both soluble and insoluble. The thin bran layer surrounds the endosperm, the biggest part of the grain, which stores most of the kernel's carbohydrate or food energy.

A tiny but very important part of the grain is the germ or embryo. This is the heart of the grain, the portion that abounds with vitamins, minerals and essential fatty acids. Unfortunately this wealthy portion is often removed during milling and refining, along with the bran as its oils can become rancid during storage. In the case of wheat, for example, this results in a pure-looking white product that is often enriched with just a fraction of the original vitamins and minerals, to partially compensate for what has been removed.

In North America and Europe, grains such as oatmeal and flaked and puffed cereals have primarily been associated with breakfast. However, many delicious and distinctively flavored grains can take a central place at lunch and dinner, as they do around the world. The grains used in the majority of our recipes are unrefined for maximum nutrition.

General guidelines for cooking grains

The size of pot used for cooking cereal grains is important. For small quantities, a small deep pot ensures that the grain is covered by water for as long as possible before it absorbs all the water. When cooking grains, the lid should be tight-fitting since all the water needs to be absorbed and evaporation needs to be kept to a minimum.

Generally speaking, grains take less time to cook than legumes and do not require pre-soaking. Always bring water to a boil before adding grains. (Cold water will draw some of the starch from grains into the surrounding water. When brought to a boil, the starch slightly thickens the water, resulting in a sticky final product. This is particularly true for grains that have had the bran removed such as white basmati rice.) Once the water has come to a boil, add the grain, cover the pot and wait for the water to return to the boil before reducing the heat to simmer.

The matter of whether to add salt to the cooking water is personal. As a rule of thumb, salt the water (if using salt), before the grains are added to the pot. This will allow the grain an opportunity to absorb salt as it cooks.

Grains are cooked when all the water has been absorbed and when the grain is soft and no longer crunchy. If the cooking temperature is too high and too much water is lost through evaporation, add a small amount of boiling water to the pot to complete the cooking. Do not stir grains while they are cooking or immediately afterward while the grain is hot: grains bruise very easily and stirring will make them sticky. Once the grain is cooked, allow the pot to rest for 5 minutes off the heat before serving. If any water remains in the bottom of the pot, drain it off.

Some grains will undoubtedly suit your liking more than others and will become staples in your household. Since grains have slightly different nutritional profiles, eating a variety ensures a wide range of nutrient intake.

The chart on page 196 is based on 1 cup (250 mL) of grain. Generally speaking 1 cup (250 mL) of dry grain will yield 2 servings; however, this depends on how hungry the eaters are and the other foods being served. Leftover grains can be easily reheated or incorporated into soups, salads, International Roll-Ups and grain puddings.

Grain	Water	Cooking Time	Yield
Amaranth	3 cups (750 mL)	25 min.	2-1/2 cups (625 mL)
Barley, pearl	4 cups (1 L)	50-60 min.	4 cups (1 L)
Buckwheat	2 cups (500 mL)	12-15 min.	4 cups (1 L)
Bulgur	2-1/2 cups [boiling water] (625 mL)	let stand 20-30 min.	3 cups (750 mL)
Cornmeal, yellow	4 cups (1 L)	5-10 min.	4-1/2 cups (1.125 L)
Millet	2-1/2 cups (625 mL)	25 min.	4 cups (1 L)
Oats, quick-cooking	2 cups (500 mL)	2-3 min.	2-1/4 cups (560 mL)
Oats, rolled	2-1/2 cups (625 mL)	20 min.	2-1/4 cups (560 mL)
Quinoa	1-1/2 cups (375 mL)	15-20 min.	3-1/2 cups (875 mL)
Rice, brown basmati	2 cups (500 mL)	40 min.	3-1/4 cups (800 mL)
Rice, brown short-grain	2 cups (500 mL)	45 min.	3-1/2 cups (875 mL)
Rice, brown long-grain	2 cups (500 mL)	45 min.	3-1/2 cups (875 mL)
Rice, white basmati	1-3/4 cups (475 mL)	18-20 min.	3 cups (750 mL)
Wheat berries	3-1/2 cups (875 mL)	50-60 min.	3 cups (750 mL)
Wild rice, whole	4 cups (1 L)	50-60 min.	3 cups (750 mL)

LEGUMES:
PLANT POWERHOUSES

Legumes form the second most important source of food to humans after cereal grains. Highly nutritious, legumes are plants with seeds in pods, and are the protein powerhouses of the plant kingdom. The dried edible seeds of legumes are more accurately called pulses, however these seeds are also commonly referred to as legumes.

Why presoak beans and peas?

When beans are harvested they have a high percentage of moisture. Bringing beans to market requires that they be dried to prolong their shelf life. Once dried, beans can be stored for years. Soaking overnight reconstitutes beans to that point when they were harvested and considerably reduces their cooking time.

In addition, soaking draws out of the legumes some of the carbohydrates that are not digested well in the small intestine. These carbohydrates pass through to the large intestine where they are acted upon by naturally occurring bacteria. A byproduct of this bacterial activity is intestinal gas, which, in excessive amounts, can produce discomfort in the lower bowel and be embarrassing. Discarding the soaking liquid and rinsing beans before they are cooked goes a long way toward reducing intestinal gas. For further information on this topic turn to "The Gas Crisis: International Solutions" in Chapter 7 of *Becoming Vegetarian*.

Furthermore, when legumes are soaked, their minerals become more available for our use. Calcium, iron, and zinc are released from a mineral-phosphate complex, allowing more of these and other minerals to be absorbed by the body. Thus more value is extracted from reconstituted beans than from beans that are cooked from a dry state.

Small beans such as mung beans, peas and lentils do not have to be soaked before cooking. Their smaller size allows them to cook more quickly than larger beans such as kidney beans and garbanzo beans (also called chick-peas). If you have the time and wish to capitalize on the increased bioavailability that soaking produces, by all means soak the small legumes as well before cooking them.

Depending on the source of the legumes you buy, you may need to pick them over before soaking to remove any twigs, pieces of dirt or small stones from the field. To do this, spread them on a baking sheet and remove unwanted bits. If peas or lentils are not going to be presoaked, rinse them to remove any dust.

A general rule of thumb for soaking legumes is to cover them with triple their volume of water for at least 6 hours or overnight. Legumes will expand between 2 and 3 times their dried volume so make sure the bowl or pot you use is large enough. Follow the directions below under "General cooking guidelines".

Quick soaking procedure

If you haven't pre-soaked legumes you can still salvage your plans for a bean-based dinner.

Wash and rinse the beans and place them in a pot. Add triple the amount of water, bring to a boil, cover, reduce the heat to low and simmer for 5 minutes. Remove the pot from heat and let rest for 1 hour. Then cook until soft according to the directions below.

General cooking guidelines

Discard the soaking liquid, rinse the beans and cover with triple the amount of fresh cold water. Bring the legumes to boil in a covered pot, then reduce the heat to simmer. Simmering the legumes is important, as boiling reduces the water too quickly and also bursts the skins.

Some legumes produce a foam in the water after it comes to a boil. Skim off the foam once or twice using a ladle. The remaining foam will eventually disappear.

Keep pot lid tilted slightly to the side to prevent the water from spilling over and allow the steam to escape.

If the water does reduce before the legumes are cooked, simply add a bit more to cover the beans by 1/2 inch (1 cm). Return the lid to the tilted position and continue cooking.

Do not add salt at the beginning of the cooking process. Salt and acidic products such as tomatoes, wine, vinegar, citrus juices or sweeteners toughen the outer skin of legumes. This makes it more difficult for water to penetrate the legume and thus increases cooking time.

Legumes are cooked when they're no longer crunchy when bitten. Test a few beans since some may be cooked before others.

Let the beans cool in their cooking liquid. This keeps their skins from splitting as a result of coming into contact with the cooler air.

Is salt needed when cooking beans?

This depends on your preference. Adding a small amount of salt (1/4 tsp/1 mL) toward the end of cooking develops the overall flavor of legumes and decreases the need for salt when adjusting the dish's final seasoning.

Do mountain dwellers need to cook longer?

Yes; at sea level, the boiling point of water is 212°F (100°C) and at higher elevations the boiling point is lower, thus requiring more time to cook and bake.

LEGUMES CHART

All yields are based on 1 cup (250 mL) of legumes and 3 cups (750 mL) of cooking water and reflect a 6-hour soaking time, except for the lentils and split peas. Note that cooking times can vary considerably depending on the age, size and variety of the legume.

Beans	Cooking Time	Approx. Yield
aduki beans	35–45 min.	3 cups (750 mL)
black beans	45–55 min.	2-1/2 cups (625 mL)
black-eyed peas	45–60 min.	2 cups (500 mL)
garbanzo beans (chick-peas)	45 min.	2-3/4 cups (675 mL)
great northern beans	45 min.	2-2/3 cups (650 mL)
kidney beans	35 min.	2-1/2 cups (625 mL)
lentils, brown	25–35 min.	2-1/4 cups (550 mL)
lentils, red	20 min.	2 cups (500 mL)
lima beans, small	55–60 min.	3 cups (750 mL)
mung beans	25–30 min.	3 cups (750 mL)
navy beans	50–60 min.	2-2/3 cups (650 mL)
pinto beans	45 min.	2-2/3 cups (650 mL)
split peas	45–60 min.	2 cups (500 mL)

SOURCES FOR INGREDIENTS AND EQUIPMENT

The following companies provide high-quality natural foods and ingredients that we use in our kitchens. We recommend that you investigate these products and begin incorporating them into your cooking.

Bob's Red Mill
5209 S.E. International Way
Milwaukie, Oregon 97222
Phone: (503) 654-3215   Fax: (503) 653-1339

An incredible array of packaged ground grains, beans, seeds, pancake mixes and more. Everything is ground with a 4,000 lb stone. Also amidst the selection of products are xanthan gum, specialty beans, cereals, lecithin granules . . . the list goes on. Top quality and delicious.

Eden Foods
701 Tecumseh Road
Clinton, Michigan 49236
Phone: (517) 456-7424   Fax: (517) 456-7025

Eden Foods is a natural food manufacturer, trader and contract grower of organically grown and traditional food. About 130 Eden brand products, including Edensoy Beverage, Eden Organic Pasta, beans, tomatoes, and exceptional imported foods are sold throughout Canada and the United States.

Frontier Cooperative Herbs
3021 78th Street
Norway, Iowa 52318
Phone: 1-800-786-1388

Member-owned since 1976, Frontier is a manufacturer and supplier of natural and organic products which include non-irradiated herbs and spices, organic coffee, tea, natural remedies and aromatherapy goods.

GrainWorks Inc.
Box 30
Vulcan, Alberta ToL 2Bo
Phone: (403) 485-2808   Fax: (403) 485-6459

GrainWorks is a certified organic 2,200-acre farm with its production based in Southern Alberta. Their product line expanded to include items from other certified organic farms. Current list has over 100 certified organic products.

Imagine Foods
350 Cambridge Avenue, Suite 350
Palo Alto, California 94306
Phone: (415) 327-1444

Imagine foods specializes in vegan and non-dairy products derived from rice, including: Rice Dream Beverage, Rice Dream Frozen Desserts and Imagine Pudding Snacks. Imagine also offers Ken and Robert's Veggie Pockets – hand-held vegetarian entrées in an organic crust – available in ten international flavors.

Lundberg Family Farms
5370 Church Street
Richvale, California 95974-0369
Phone: (916) 882-4551   Fax: (916) 882-4500

Lundberg rice and rice products such as entrées, cereals, puddings, rice cakes and rice syrups are top quality. The growing and processing techniques of Lundberg Family Farms have developed out of the family's deep-rooted beliefs about the land and surrounding ecology.

Mori-Nu Tofu

2050 W. 190th Street, Suite 110

Torrance, California 90504

Phone: (604) 254-8888 (Canadian distributor)

Phone: (310) 787-0200 (US manufacturer)   Fax: (310) 787-2727

This company provides Mori-Nu silken tofu as well as the world's lowest fat tofu, Mori Nu Lite; both are available in soft, firm and extra firm. Mori-Nu's revolutionary aseptic package keeps this tofu fresh without refrigeration, preservatives or irradiation for months! Its versatile, creamy, smooth texture provides a vegetable protein alternative to milk, cream, cheese and eggs in thousands of recipes.

Muir Glen Organic Tomato Products

424 North 7th Street

Sacramento, California 95814

Phone: (800) 832-6345   Fax: (916) 557-0903

Muir Glen Organic Tomato Products offers a full line of canned organic tomato products, including juice, ketchup, sauce, diced, ground peeled and whole peeled tomatoes; plus a full line of glass-packed pasta sauces and salsas.

Nature's Path Foods Inc.

7453 Progress Way

Delta, B.C. V4G 1E8

Phone: (604) 940-2261   Fax: (604) 940-0522

Nature's Path Foods Inc. is a Canadian company that produces certified organic and exceptionally delicious breakfast cereals, breads and sesame tahini. Based in Vancouver, Nature's Path has a full distribution in Canada and the U.S.A.

Omega Nutrition Canada Inc.

1924 Franklin Street

Vancouver, B.C. V5L 1R2

Phone: (800) 661-3529

e-mail: Omega_Nutrition@mindlink.bc.ca

Omega Nutrition manufactures certified organic, unrefined Omegaflo salad and cooking oils. The Omegaflo process protects the extremely delicate essential fatty acids naturally present in seeds and nuts from destructive light, heat and oxygen.

Red Star Yeast & Products
A Division of Universal Foods Corporation
P.O. Box 737
Milwaukee, Wisconsin 53202
Phone: (414) 271-6755
Producers of Red Star Vegetarian Support Formula nutritional yeast specifically developed for vegetarians. Vegetarian Support Formula contains minerals and B vitamins, including a reliable source of vitamin B12.

Saskatchewan Pulse Crop Development Board
210 - 111 Research Drive
Saskatoon, Saskatchewan S7N 3R2
Phone: (306) 668-5558   Fax: (306) 668-5557
The Saskatchewan Pulse Crop Development Board represents the province's lentil, pea, bean and chickpea producers. Although the board does not market pulses, it supports the pulse industry in the areas of research, extension and market development.

Sunrise Soya Foods
733 Powell Street
Vancouver, B.C. V6A 1H5
Phone: (604) 254-8888
As Canada's leading tofu company, Sunrise manufactures and distributes a full line of tofu, soya beverages and other types of soya foods. These products can be used as highly nutritious substitutes for meat, poultry, eggs or dairy.

Sucanat North America Corporation
26 Clinton Drive, # 117
Hollis, New Hampshire 03049
Phone: (603) 595-2922   Fax: (603) 595-2923

Sucanat (*sugar cane natural*) is a tasty golden brown sugar derived from 100% evaporated cane juice made from freshly squeezed sugar cane juice. Because nothing is added and only water is removed, Sucanat retains the vitamins, minerals and trace elements found naturally in the sugar cane plant. Sucanat may be used as a one-for-one replacement for white refined or brown sugar.

Yves Veggie Cuisine
1638 Derwent Way
Delta, B.C. V3M 6R9
Phone: (604) 525-1345   Fax: (604) 525-2555

Yves Veggie Cuisine manufactures a full line of tasty, nutritious and easy to prepare award-winning food products that are made from vegetable protein. They are low in saturated fat, cholesterol free and contain no preservatives or artificial ingredients. The company's product line includes three basic categories: burgers, patties, wieners, and slices.

Green Power Juice Extractor
Green Power International
12020 Woodruff Ave., Suite C
Dowdney, California 90241
Phone: (888) 254-7336 or (310) 940-4241
Fax: (310) 940-4240

This juicer can produce not only the superb "Vegan Dass Ice Cream" on page 192, but also fruit and vegetable juices that retain top nutritional quality, as well as baby food, nut butters and pasta.

International ProSoya Corporation
312 – 19292 60th Avenue
Surrey, B.C. V3S 8E5
Phone: (604) 532-8030
Fax: (604) 534-2060

Makers of the *So Nice* brand of soy products.

SELECTED REFERENCES

Becoming Vegetarian by Vesanto Melina, Brenda Davis and Victoria Harrison, Macmillan Canada, 1995.

Diet, Nutrition and Prevention of Chronic Diseases. World Health Organization Study Group on Diet, Nutrition and Prevention of Non-communicable Diseases. Geneva, Switzerland Technical Report Series No. 797. World Health Organization, 1991.

Eco-Cuisine by Ron Pickarski, Ten Speed Press, Berkeley, California.

Famous Vegetarians and Their Favorite Recipes by Rynn Berry, Pythagorean Publishers, New York.

Friendly Foods by Ron Pickarski, Ten Speed Press, Berkeley, California.

Plant proteins in relation to human protein and amino acid nutrition. Young, V.R. and Pellett, P.L. American Journal of Clinical Nutrition volume 59 (supplement), pages 1203S–1212S, 1994.

Table for Two by Joanne Stepaniak, The Book Publishing Company, Summertown, Tennessee.

The Moosewood Cookbook by Mollie Katzen, Ten Speed Press, Berkeley, California.

The Uncheese Cookbook by Joanne Stepaniak, The Book Publishing Company, Summertown, Tennessee.

INDEX